PSYCHOLOGY OF THE ASSOCIATED MINDS

Carlo Cattaneo

Original title: *Psicologia delle menti associate*
Copyright © 2016 Istituto Lombardo di Scienze e Lettere

Translator: David Gibbons
Typesetting: Laura Panigara, Cesano Boscone (MI)

Copyright © 2019 Bocconi University Press
             EGEA S.p.A.

EGEA S.p.A.
Via Salasco, 5 - 20136 Milano
Tel. 02/5836.5751 – Fax 02/5836.5753
egea.edizioni@unibocconi.it – www.egeaeditore.it

All rights reserved, including but not limited to translation, total or partial adaptation, reproduction, and communication to the public by any means on any media (including microfilms, films, photocopies, electronic or digital media), as well as electronic information storage and retrieval systems. For more information or permission to use material from this text, see the website www.egeaeditore.it

Given the characteristics of Internet, the publisher is not responsible for any changes of address and contents of the websites mentioned.

First edition: August 2019

ISBN Domestic Edition	978-88-99902-56-8
ISBN International Edition	978-88-85486-88-1
ISBN Epub and Mobipocket International Edition	978-88-85486-89-8

Table of Content

Abbreviations, Sources and Bibliographical Details	VII
Cattaneo as Modern Philosopher by *Carlo G. Lacaita*	1
Introduction to this Edition by *Barbara Boneschi*	29
Biography of Cattaneo's Life	37
List of Texts	49
Lecture I. Idea of a Psychology of the Sciences	**53**
Notes	53
Text	56
Lecture II. On the Formation of Systems	**67**
Notes	67
Text	71
Lecture III. On Antithesis as a Method of Social Psychology	**81**
Notes	81
Text	84
Lecture IV. On Sensation in Associated Minds	**95**
Notes	95
Text	98
Lectures V and VI – On Analysis in Associated Minds	**103**
Notes	103

Lecture V. On Analysis in Associated Minds. Part I — 108
   Text — 108

Lecture VI. On Analysis in Associated Minds. Part II — 115
   Text — 115

APPENDIXES

Psychology of Associated Minds. Preface — 133
   Notes — 133
   Text — 134

Psychology of the Solitary Mind. Second Psychology or the History of Associated Minds. Outline or Contents — 145
   Notes — 145
   Text — 147

Bibliography — 151

Index of Names — 159

List of Figures — 163

Abbreviations, Sources and Bibliographical Details

ACM — Archivio Carlo Cattaneo, Civiche raccolte storiche, Comune di Milano. The inventory of the Archive edited by the Office of Raccolte storiche Comune di Milano, is in *Le carte di Carlo Cattaneo, Catalogo*, foreword by Leopoldo Marchetti, Milano, 1951.

AIL — Archivio of Istituto Lombardo Accademia di Scienze e Lettere, Milano.

IL — Istituto Lombardo Accademia di Scienze e Lettere.

AS — *Alcuni scritti del dottor Carlo Cattaneo,* Milano, Borroni e Scotti, 3 voll., 1846-47.

ATTI IL — *Atti del Reale Istituto Lombardo di Scienze, Lettere ed Arti*, Milano, Tipografia Bernardoni.

RENDICONTI IL — *Rendiconti del Reale Istituto Lombardo di Scienze e Lettere*, dal 1864 in two volumes, one for *Classe di Lettere e Scienze morali e politiche*, and the other for *Classe di Scienze matematiche e naturali*, Milano, Tipografia Bernardoni.

OEI — *Opere edite ed inedite di Carlo Cattaneo. Raccolte da Agostino Bertani e ordinate per cura degli amici suoi*, Firenze, Le Monnier, 1881-1892, 7 vols.; vols. VI e VII correspond to vols. I and II of the *Scritti di filosofia*, Firenze, Le Monnier, 1892, collected and edited by Alberto Mario e Niccola Mameli.

SPE — CARLO CATTANEO, *Scritti politici ed epistolario*, edited by Gabriele Rosa e Jessie White Mario, Firenze, Barbera, 1892-1901, 3 vols.

FFC — CARLO CATTANEO, *Frammenti di filosofia civile, ed. milanese riordinata da Arcangelo Ghisleri secondo la mente dell'autore, Milano*, Edizioni Risorgimento, 1926.

EP — *Epistolario di Carlo Cattaneo*, collected and annotated by Rinaldo Caddeo, Firenze, Barbèra, 1949-1956, 4 vols.

SE	CARLO CATTANEO, *Scritti economici*, edited by Alberto Bertolino, Firenze, Le Monnier, 1956, 3 vols.
SSG	CARLO CATTANEO, *Scritti storici e geografici*, edited by Gaetano Salvemini e Ernesto Sestan, Firenze, Le Monnier, 1957-1967, 4 vols.
SF	CARLO CATTANEO, *Scritti filosofici*, edited by Norberto Bobbio, Firenze, Le Monnier, 1960, 3 vols.
SEI	CARLO CATTANEO, *Scritti sull'educazione e sull'istruzione*, edited by Luigi Ambrosoli, Firenze, La Nuova Italia, 1963.
SP	CARLO CATTANEO, *Scritti politici*, edited by Mario Boneschi, Firenze, Le Monnier, 1964-1965, 4 vols.
SST	CARLO CATTANEO, *Scritti scientifici e tecnici,* edited by Carlo G. Lacaita, t.I, Firenze, Giunti-G. Barbèra, 1969, (planned in several vols. but only the first was plubished).
OPS	CARLO CATTANEO, *Opere scelte*, edited by Delia Castelnuovo Frigessi, Torino, Einaudi, 1972, 4 vols.
SL	CARLO CATTANEO, *Scritti letterari*, edited by Delia Castelnuovo Frigessi, Torino, Einaudi, 1972, 4 vols.
TO	CARLO CATTANEO, *Tutte le opere*, edited by Luigi Ambrosoli, 2 vols.; Milan: Mondadori, 1967-74.
NNCL	CARLO CATTANEO, *Notizie naturali e civili su la Lombardia*, edited by G. Bigatti, Firenze, Le Monnier, Bellinzona, Casagrande, 2 vols., 2014.
PMA-EC	CARLO CATTANEO, *Psicologia delle menti associate. Le letture di Carlo Cattaneo all'Istituto Lombardo di Scienze e Lettere,* critical edition by Barbara Boneschi, Istituto Lombardo di Scienze e Lettere, Milano, 2016.
CARTEGGI SI	*Carteggi di Carlo Cattaneo*, Serie I, *Lettere di Carlo Cattaneo*, edited by Margherita Cancarini Petroboni e Mariachiara Fugazza, Firenze, Le Monnier; Bellinzona, Edizioni Casagrande, 2001, 2005, 2010, 3 vols.
CARTEGGI SII	*Carteggi di Carlo Cattaneo*, Serie II, *Lettere dei corrispondenti,* edited by Carlo Agliati, Firenze, Le Monnier; Bellinzona, Edizioni Casagrande, 2001-2005, 2 vols.
BC	*La biblioteca di Carlo Cattaneo*, edited by Carlo G. Lacaita, Raffaella Gobbo e Alfredo Turiel, Bellinzona, Edizioni Casagrande, 2003.
ILASL-I	*L'Istituto Lombardo Accademia di Scienze e Lettere, (secoli XIX-XX), I-Storia istituzionale*, edited by Adele Robbiati Bianchi, Milano, Istituto Lombardo Accademia di Scienze e Lettere, Libri Scheiwiller, 2007.

Abbreviations, Sources and Bibliographical Details

ILASL-II — *L'Istituto Lombardo Accademia di Scienze e Lettere, (secoli XIX-XX), II-Storia della Classe di Scienze matematiche e naturali*, edited by Emilio Gatti e Adele Robbiati Bianchi, Milano, Istituto Lombardo Accademia di Scienze e Lettere, Libri Scheiwiller, 2008.

ILASL-III — *L'Istituto Lombardo Accademia di Scienze e Lettere, (secoli XIX-XX), III-Storia della Classe di Scienze morali*, edited by Maurizio Vitale, Giovanni Orlandi e Adele Robbiati Bianchi, Milano, Istituto Lombardo Accademia di Scienze e Lettere, Libri Scheiwiller, 2009.

Annali — "Annali universali di Statistica", Francesco Lampato, Milano.

Bollettino — "Bollettino di notizie statistiche ed economiche italiane e straniere e delle più importanti invenzioni o scoperte, e progresso dell'industria e delle utili cognizioni", Francesco Lampato, Milano.

Il Politecnico — "Il Politecnico, Repertorio mensile di studj applicati alla prosperità e coltura sociale", Milano, Pirola Luigi di Pirola Giacomo, from 1/1839 to 6/1844; Editori del Politecnico, Tip. Pietro Agnelli, from 1/1860 to 12/1865; the indexes of the Journal are ordered in *"Il Politecnico" di Carlo Cattaneo. La vicenda editoriale, i collaboratori, gli indici*, edited by Carlo G. Lacaita, Raffaella Gobbo, Enzo R. Laforgia, Marina Priano, Foreword by Carlo G. Lacaita, Lugano, Giampiero Casagrande Editore, 2005.

Other abbreviations

a. — *anno* (year)

cart. — *cartella* (folder)

cf. — compare (Latin *confer*)

ch. — chapter

fasc. — *fascicolo* (file)

ff. — following

ms(s) — manuscript(s)

no. — number/numbers

op. cit — work cited (*opus citatum*)

p./pp. — page/pages

pl. — *plico* (envelope)

vol./vols — volume/volumes

Cattaneo as Modern Philosopher

di *Carlo G. Lacaita*

Carlo Cattaneo was an analytical thinker and a socially committed writer, a careful observer of contemporary changes, and an enthusiastic advocate of forward-thinking projects inspired by universal values. In the course of his career he was responsible for a vast number of articles and essays. Collecting his writings has proved to be a laborious process, as they were published in a wide variety of different periodicals, often unsigned and in some cases not published at all.

It is no surprise, then, that towards the end of his life, on more than one occasion he expressed regret at having used so much of his energies in journalistic activities and editing collective publications, rather than bringing the fruits of his learning together in more systematic form. Scholars of his work, however, have increasingly recognized that the plethora of his writings does in fact contain an organic system of thought, full of profound observations and at times brilliant insights. The first to acknowledge this were his disciples, who republished many of his writings near the end of the nineteenth century, followed by his some of his best-known advocates, such as Gaetano Salvemini, Alessandro Levi and Norberto Bobbio (to name but a few). His *Psychology of Associated Minds* provides an eloquent testimony to the calibre of his thinking. This is one of the main reasons why we have chosen to make it available to a wider readership, to coincide with the one hundred and fiftieth anniversary of Cattaneo's death, by publishing for the first time an English translation of the critical edition curated by Barbara Boneschi for the *Istituto Lombardo Accademia di Scienze e Lettere* in 2016.

The *Psychology of Associated Minds* consists of a series of six "readings", or lectures, delivered in the years between 1859 and 1866, plus various summaries destined for more rapid forms of diffusion. It represents the final expression of a system that Cattaneo had been developing for some four decades, based around a theoretical nucleus he had constructed in the years of his intellectual formation. During the Habsburg Restoration in Milan, the teachings of the Lombard enlightenment published in *Il Caffè* by Cesare Beccaria and the Verri brothers were still very much current, fused with Giambattista Vico's historicism. It was this combination which encouraged the young Cattaneo to start his research into natural and human reality in its most diverse aspects.

In his autobiographical memories, of which there is no shortage in his writings and letters, Cattaneo pointed out on several occasions how his family environment encouraged his early curiosity and voracious reading, by supplying him with works such as Livy's *History of Rome*, giving him an opportunity to read "the entire collection of De La Harpe's journeys", and allowing him free access to the extensive holdings of the Biblioteca Ambrosiana and the Gabinetto Numismatico in Brera, the latter held some "twelve thousand volumes of ancient and modern history, literature, fine arts, travel, customs and erudite and unusual languages".[1] Of the teachers encountered in the course of his studies, the ones he recalled with most fondness were those who had directed him towards the study of languages as "the work of generations, and a monument of what happened to them";[2] those who had opened his mind "to the idea of the Middle Ages, the vast world of Asia, and the other sources excluded from the circle of ancient studies";[3] and those who had assisted him in the scientific study of nature, and had taught him the importance of technological progress.[4]

The decisive encounter for Cattaneo, as he himself said on several occasions, was with legal scholar and philosopher Gian Domenico Romagnosi. Cattaneo met Romagnosi in 1820, when he decided to pursue his studies privately rather than attend law courses at the University of Pavia, a decision that allowed him to combine his research with teaching grammar classes at a local high school, and so become financially independent from his family. This decision meant he would abandon "the law forever to pursue research",[5] allowing him

---

[1] *SP*, III, pp. 302-3.
[2] *SL*, I, p. 280.
[3] *SSG*, III, 51.
[4] On the young Cattaneo's education, see Sestan, (1951, pp. 209-42), and Ambrosoli, (1960, pp. 15-40). Cf. further comments in *BC*, and the extensive notes in the first volumes of Cattaneo's correspondence: *Carteggi SI* and *Carteggi SII*.
[5] *EP*, IV, pp. 102-3. In noting Cattaneo's "departure" from Romagnosi, Sestan, in his "Introduction" (1957), downplays Romagnosi's role in the education of his favourite student. Closer to the expressions of esteem and affection which we find throughout Cattaneo's writings, right to the end, is the opinion of Ambrosoli (1960, pp. 25-6).

to broaden his reading in thoroughly diverse directions. In this way, even after graduating in 1824, he was able to continue in dialogue with some very lively cultural *milieux*, not least that of his beloved teacher, who combined the legacy of the Enlightenment with the European dimension of the Napoleonic period and the insurrectionary aspirations of the Risorgimento.[6] Working closely with Romagnosi, Cattaneo acquired the habit of applying the scientific method to investigating the various aspects of community or, as he called it, "associated" life, identifying the connections and distinctions between ethics, law and economics, aiming in particular to "combine law and economics, subjecting the claims of interest to the restraint of the law, and the assertions of law to the approval of interest".[7] He came to espouse his teacher's vision, which they shared with Beccaria and Bentham, of punishment not as a form of revenge but "defence", to be achieved as painlessly as possible and for preventative and rehabilitative purposes".[8] He absorbed the idea that the ability to be "perfected" is a typical characteristic of humankind, noting the importance of institutions and cultural and political systems in the collective advancement of humanity on the road to civilization.

At the same time, as Cattaneo's first work (on Romagnosi's *Assunto primo della scienza del diritto naturale*, written while still a university student in 1822) shows he was already in the process of defining what were to become the pillars of his own political thought: the principle of liberty (in the sense of autonomy), the principle of equality ("all men are equal, that is to say, their rights are equally inviolable"), and the related idea of power being limited by citizens' "native" rights.[9] This idea was linked to another, also present in Romagnosi's works, of the state as a form of "negotiation", able to acknowledge the plurality of its various internal constituents, to encourage peaceful coexistence, and to spread "social value" to the highest possible number of cohabitants.[10]

Philosophically Cattaneo was educated in the "cult of Locke and Bonnet", and soon attained the conviction that in order for human knowledge to de-

---

[6] On Romagnosi and his "civil philosophy" cf. Albertoni (1979); and Albertoni (1990). On Romagnosi and Cattaneo cf. Lacaita, (1983, pp. 585-614), and Ghiringhelli, (2004, pp. 317-23).

[7] *SE*, I, pp. 180-81.

[8] *SP*, I, 288. Elsewhere, on the need for crime prevention which both Romagnosi and Bentham had emphasized, he wrote that "punishment is a remedy of the utmost necessity and degenerates into gratuitous violence when all the other forces that prevent evil have not been deployed" (*SE*, I, p. 317).

[9] *SF*, I, pp. 8-11.

[10] *SF*, I, p. 162.

velop properly, it must be based on experience and free reason, starting from factual evidence and ascending from there to principles, and from specific principles to general ones, all the time checking that they continue to remain valid.

In the same period Cattaneo was also digesting Vico's important approach to history (Romagnosi published his *Osservazioni su La Scienza Nuova di Vico* in 1822[11]), and considering how to look at all different expressions of humankind, from widespread beliefs to ethical and legal norms, from techniques of labour to ritual ceremonies, as social and collective constructions rather than as the work of isolated individuals.

In was in the 1820s, then, that the young Cattaneo came to see the passage from individual to society as a philosophical watershed, a change of perspective which, while emphasizing the active role played by individuals with "power and conscience",[12] caused him to see life in association as indispensable for an understanding of humanity, history and civilization. It was in living together with their peers that human beings were emancipated from their initial "state of feral stupidity and mortal weakness",[13] he wrote as early as 1822, and were able to develop "their own faculties"; to increase their wealth of knowledge and ability to use natural resources;[14] and to complete the transition from one level of culture to a more advanced one, that is, "from the most shapeless society, gradually to the most sophisticated one".[15] Thus if we are to study humanity, Cattaneo would soon argue, it is no longer sufficient to look merely at the individual conscience, as Descartes and Condillac, Locke and Bonnet had done, but all its expressions as seen "in histories, languages, religions, arts and sciences" must be analysed,[16] through the critical and empirical observation which is typical of modern experimentalism, applied systematically to the multi-faceted world of humanity, as modern science had already shown it was capable of doing with nature, and productively so.

Fascinated by the many themes that history and civilization offered for reflection, the young Cattaneo chose not to build on his journalistic debut in 1822, but to continue instead with further analysis of these issues. Evidence of his decision may be found in the outline compiled in 1824 for an essay,

---

[11] It was published in *L'Ape Italiana* in 1822 and republished in vol. II of Romagnosi's *Opere* edited by De Giorgi; now it may be found in Romagnosi, (1974, pp. 19-36).

[12] Already in his first article published in 1822 he had written that: "man, in associating with his peers, does not condemn himself to being an individual non-entity" (*SF*, I, p. 6).

[13] *SF*, I, p. 6.
[14] *SF*, I, pp. 7-8.
[15] *SF*, I, p. 4.
[16] *SF*, I, p. 53.

which was never completed, on the influence of the great barbarian transmigration on the Italian language (*Influenza della gran trasmigrazione di barbari sulla lingua italiana*), which contains several clues as to "the course followed by his thoughts"[17] and the principles he was establishing at the time. These range from the "mixed origin of all languages", and hence of all nations (in the sense of historical and cultural realities born from the coming together of different populations and cultures, coexisting or mingleing with each other), to relations between the ancient and Romance languages; from the "mixed origins of the primitive Italian languages" to the "first spread of a common language"; from the "Etruscan federation" to the "formation of the feudal system"; from development of the city states in Upper and Middle Italy to the struggles between Guelfs and Ghibellines; from the "formation of the national language" ("the Italian language was established quickly; but its use spread slowly, from subject to subject") to the "action and reaction between language and dialects", demonstrating their original variety; from the religious, agricultural, artisan, commercial and warfaring "ideas" present in Italy after the invasions, to the "destruction of feudalism" and the "resurgence of cities" towards the end of the Middle Ages.

These are all themes and issues which Cattaneo would discuss further in due course.[18] In the meantime, however, the young scholar was immersed in studying, with Romagnosi, on his own or with others, the works of Condorcet, Genovesi, Herder, Schlegel, Smith, Ferguson, Stellini, Pagano, Destutt de Tracy, Bentham, Jannelli, Sismondi and Guizot, and also those of Hobbes, Machiavelli, Hume, Benjamin Constant and many other authors, ancient and modern. Most of these works he borrowed from Romagnosi's library and acquired after his teacher's death, to have them with him at all times. Cattaneo himself contributed to the publication of one of them, the Italian translation of William Robertson's *An Historical Disquisition Concerning the Knowledge which the Ancients had of India* (*Ricerche storiche sull'India antica*, 1827), to which Ro-

---

[17] *SL*, I, p. 249.
[18] Cf., for example, his essay on the "Vita di Dante di Cesare Balbo", published in *Il Politecnico* in 1839, in which Cattaneo speaks of "Italian civilization", of "nation" and "literature", of languages and dialects, and emphasizes the diversity that comes "from the difference between the primitive populations, which never uprooted themselves from their native terrain, neither after the Romans nor before them; and which, in taking over the Latin tongue from the Romans, modified according to their former language, whether this be Etruscan or Celtic, Venetian or Carnic, and to their domestic way of pronouncing it. The later invasions did not introduce even one element to some dialect or another that was not equally introduced to all of them, and earlier still in the written language" (*SL*, I, pp. 117-18).

magnosi had added "supplementary notes and illustrations" from German cartographer and traveller Carsten Niebuhr's account of his *Travels through Arabia, and other Countries in the East* that Cattaneo had obtained for his teacher.[19]

But the civilization which Cattaneo studied so seriously with Romagnosi and the rest of his circle was not only a wide-ranging subject for research and reflection. It was also a field of action, in which all people of culture were called to make their contribution for the good of collective progress in the different areas of social life. Indeed, when Cattaneo felt the time had come, he began his activity as journalist, writing for the *Annali universali di statistica*, a review in which the debate primarily regarded how to "keep up with universal progress". He did this by emphasizing the changes achieved in other countries that were possible in Italy as well, discussing for the most part themes that were specific and practical, such as "railways, legislative reforms, tariffs, and banks":[20] not only were such issues less affected by censorship, they were also ideal for discussion with the most dynamic of social forces.[21]

As for his philosophical or political ideas, which he was unable to express freely, this can be found by reading between the lines of his writings, for example in his recurrent use of key words such as "unity", "variety", "universality" and "difference". Thus, underpinning his 1833 essay on the issue of customs duties in the United States we perceive his democratic, federalist vision, for example when he exalts the "full liberty" granted to the "opinion of all" and condemns the slavery of blacks and the "infamous market of human beings", when he points to the federal state as the best able to combine unity and freedom, entrusting central power with the duty of "keeping the domestic and foreign peace, ensuring a uniform monetary system, protecting the sanctity of contracts, disseminating enlightenment, and performing [...] a few other functions as well",[22] leaving wide-ranging powers to the other public and private decision-making levels. Also present is the European dimension of his federalism, expressed in terms very similar to those he would use after 1848, when he affirmed that the federal system had made the United States

---

[19] Cf. *BC*, p. 29. It is worth mentioning here that Cattaneo had another learned relative by the name of Antonio Madini, a "distinguished orientalist" (*EP*, IV, p. 478), who published *Il Segistan, ovvero Il corso del fiume Hindmend secondo Abu Ishak-el-Farssi-el-Isstachri geografo arabo* (Milan: Bernardoni, 1842). On the early nineteenth-century Milanese cultural production that drove research on various forms of civilization, cf. Lacaita, (1995, pp. 203-19).

[20] *SP*, I, p. 31. On the importance which Cattaneo ascribed to "special" studies, see *SE*, I, p. 181.

[21] *SE*, I, pp. 22-3.

[22] *SE*, I, p. 30.

"a powerful and feared nation, rather than a herd of small, scattered colonies, envious, hostile, and forced to live with their weapons at hand the whole time, like the Europeans."[23]

No less indicative is his article on the proposed Milan-Venice railway, written in 1836. While many asserted that the shortest and most direct route was the most convenient, Cattaneo argued that the line able to attract the highest volumes of traffic in terms of people and freight, linking the highest possible number of medium-sized urban centres, was preferable, on the grounds that it was more advantageous economically even though it was longer.

The cities of Italy, Cattaneo wrote, referring back to the nation's long history, "are the ancient centres of all communications in large and populous provinces. All the roads and markets in their respective areas converge on them; they function rather like the heart in a system of veins. They are the terms to which all *consumption* is directed and from which all *industries and capital* derive. They are a point of intersection, or rather, a *centre of gravity*; and gravity, as we know, cannot be made to fall on merely any point chosen at random."[24]

In alluding to the political unity to be established in the Italian peninsula, he added another phrase that would become something of a refrain for him: "Anyone who, in Italy, fails to take account of the love of one's own individual homeland will always be sowing in the sand".[25]

Shortly after this came Cattaneo's best-known and most indepth work of his early period, the *Ricerche economiche sulle Interdizioni imposte dalla legge civile agli Israeliti* ("Economic research on the Interdictions imposed by civil law on the Jews"). The volume was written in late 1835 and dated 1836, but only appeared early in 1837, due to publication being withheld by the state censor. In it, we find the idea of human progress described as a universal process of evolution, the outworking of which not only takes manifold forms, but is also "painstaking, slow and gradual". Cattaneo asserted that the state in which a people finds itself is the result of history, showing how centuries of oppression and marginalization led the Jews to devote themselves to activities disapproved of by the very communities that had marginalized them in the first place, and

---

[23] *SE*, I, p. 52. In the *Insurrezione di Milano del 1848* he later wrote that "we will have peace when we have the United States of Europe"; and in the *Considerazioni* to the first volume of the *Archivio triennale* in 1851 he commented further: "The day that Europe [...] writes on its forehead: The United States of Europe: not only will it have withdrawn from this mournful need for battles, fires and gallows, but it will also have gained a hundred thousand million" (*SSG*, IV, p. 329 and *SSG*, II, p. 178).

[24] *SE*, I, pp. 116-17.

[25] *SE*, I, pp. 118.

arguing that their position would change if the prejudices and interdictions against them were ended. This process was already underway as a result of increased tolerance, and the steps recently made in the direction of legal equality.

Cattaneo's aversion to the interdictions still in force against this and indeed any other minority is justified by a dense series of arguments serving to demonstrate that the end of the restrictions and discriminations was in the "interests" of the societies that were imposing them. Once released from these artificial restrictions, the capital owned by the Jews would be free to "pursue opportunities", "achieve the best use, according to the optimal location and commodity",[26] in other words to increase economic development and modernize industry. The first sector in which this would take place for Cattaneo was agriculture, which still had an important role in the life of every country, in Italy particularly, but which, he argued, should now be considered against the backdrop of the industrial transformation underway in the rest of Europe, which had started to affect the Italian peninsula as well, as shown by the introduction of steam engines, the new machinery used in manufacturing, the use of gas in street lighting in city centres, the electrical telegraph in long-distance communications, and other such "sublime" inventions. In an article on "The Industry of Birmingham" written for *L'Eco della Borsa* in 1837, after illustrating the extra production capacity achieved by the British industrial system, Cattaneo argued it was possible to "compete with or resist this industrial force only by *imitating it*".[27]

For him, then, it was a matter of keeping up with, and consciously participating in, the changes of the time, to take every opportunity and use the modern capacity to generate wealth as the basis for achieving general civil and cultural progress. It was with this in mind that Cattaneo devised his most important publishing venture, *Il Politecnico*, which appeared for the first time in 1839. This journal gave Cattaneo an opportunity to give full expression to his impressive versatility, while many aspects of his developing ideology had to this point been only hinted at or kept in the background, now he could give free rein to all of them simply by exploring the full breadth offered by its title, which he lost no time in doing.

Il Politecnico gave room not only to "arts" in the sense of the sciences of physics and mathematics being applied to relations between humanity and nature, but also to "social arts" concerning human relations, to "intellectual arts", to improve our capacity to reason, and to "fine arts", to produce beauty to be enjoyed by all. After the first two half-yearly editions, he felt able to say that,

---

[26] *SF*, I, p. 244.
[27] *SST*, p. 72.

despite having devoted considerable space to the "things which are most obviously useful, such as steam, gas used for street lighting, stearin, silk worms, woodlands, soils, slaughter houses, hydraulic constructions, geological explorations, electrostatic induction, and popular medicine", during the first year of its life *Il Politecnico* had concerned itself with a great many other subjects as well. As he said: "we have discussed the education of engineers, manual workers, the deaf, dumb and blind; we have not failed to discuss research into the mind and the lofty reasons of ethics, without which prosperity of trade or the wealth of states will not endure. We have promoted historical issues, or rather, all those issues that regard the origin and progress of civilization".[28]

It was in these writings especially that the author of the *Psychology of Associated Minds* expressed the main points of his philosophy, focused on civilization, both as object of knowledge – of historical, anthropological and philosophical analysis – and field of action, to which everyone must contribute by taking an active part in the ongoing struggle "between progress and inertia, between thought and ignorance, between kindness and barbarity, and between emancipation and slavery".[29] Decisive in both cases for Cattaneo was the notion of cultural renewal, without which the ongoing process of transformation could neither be understood nor addressed, only experienced passively.

Tradition, he wrote in his journal, "may perhaps be able to direct peoples in the exercise of ancient arts very well practised, but when new arts must be learnt and competition from new industries tackled, or when the country requires to be decorated with the gifts of modern civilization, in such cases a great number of trained minds are necessary, people who are confident in their ability to handle progressive ideas. Where the number of thoroughly trained men is inadequate, it is hard for the wisest of counsels to prevail, for jealous, astute interests soon join with the multitude's prejudices and passions, causing them easily to believe that inertia is prudence, and that disdain for studies is sound practical reason".[30]

Apart from wanting the help the "multitude" approach science with its triumphs and possible applications to the "practical field", in *Il Politecnico* Cattaneo sought to promote dialogue between practitioners of the most varied disciplines and co-operation with philosophy, the purpose of the latter being to enquire into the activities of thought and discuss the results achieved in the various sectors. In turning their gaze to beyond their own field of enquiry, Cat-

---

[28] *SF*, I, p. 236.
[29] *SF*, I, p. 234.
[30] *SF*, I, p. 244.

taneo wrote, not only would such thinkers be able to draw "light from the light of others, and take example from others' paths",[31] they could also provide each other with respective "proofs of their veracity". Philosophy, in examining the paths taken and conquests made in the various disciplines, could help them refine their methods and build together the broadest synthesis "that is possible".[32]

At the same time, Cattaneo stressed the collective origins and the associative and dialectic character of human knowledge. Thus, in his essay on chemical variations for non-chemists ("Varietà chimiche pei non chimici"), the departure from dogmatic thought, which gave birth to modern science is presented as a product of the late medieval city states' renaissance, where "the Italian peoples, organized in free, wealthy, courageous and armed city states, well versed in trade with the whole continent, in sailing the distant seas, in the practices of progressive industry, civilized by popular poets and confident story tellers, […] subjected the vanity of the schools to the scourge of irony, or resolutely submitted themselves to the proof of facts and the study of nature".[33]

And even in cases – such as Lavoisier – where the role of the individual is said to be decisive in the modern transition from "qualitative" to "quantitative" analysis, he still emphasized the long, hard work that preceded it, by the Arabs in particular. Moreover, all knowledge, Cattaneo again argued, is born and develops in a social context, and the whole scientific enterprise which develops over the centuries, with contributions from different peoples and cultures, finds its truth criteria "in the intersection of dissimilar, unforeseen proofs […], not in long, risky deductions from a *first assertion*, as the ontologists claim".[34]

Inspired by the publication of his friend Giuseppe Ferrari's *Vico et l'Italie*, Cattaneo returned to the importance of Vico's *Scienza nuova*, which in his

---

[31] *SF*, I, p. 246. See also pp. 172-73.

[32] *SF*, II, p. 32.

[33] *SST*, p. 257. Cattaneo returned to the genesis of modern scientific thought on several occasions in his writings. Referring to the vitality of Florence in particular, in his well-known essay on the *City as the Ideal Principle in the Histories of Italy* published in 1858 he wrote as follows: "The Florentine artisan was the first in Europe to participate in scientific culture. The mechanical arts came to be intimately connected with the fine arts; and these with geometry, optics and physics. The Tuscan artist did not confine his genius to a single art. […] For the variety of their knowledge brought them, by psychological necessity, from the particulars of their arts and trades to the general principles of mathematical contemplation. Thus did the experimental method start to become operative in the Tuscan tradition over the course of six centuries, a method in which the eye and hand prepare the first elements of science for the intellect, and all thought is preordained not towards proud and sterile speculation, but to what Bacon later called *scientia activa*" (*SSG*, II, p. 434).

[34] *SST*, p. 268.

view had opened up the possibility of a new way of studying humanity and history. "We cannot capture the human spirit", he wrote, underlining a concept he would later develop in the *Psychology of Associated Minds*, "we cannot scrutinize its essence, we can only know it insofar as it manifests itself in acts and elaborations". Moreover, he added:

> When we have contemplated the ideological *polyhedron* in the maximum number of its countless different faces, the features common to all them will reveal its fundamental and constant nature to us; while the others will show us the varied field in which it can be perfected. These features are scattered through histories, laws, rites and languages; and from this terrain, which is thoroughly historical and *experimental*, the entire knowledge of humanity must arise, which in vain will be sought in the recesses of the solitary conscience. The study of the *individual* within humanity, *social ideology*, is the prism through which the unsteady white light of internal psychology is refracted into different, resplendent colours.[35]

Unlike Heinrich Leo, who did not take many groups of people into consideration in writing his *Universalgeschichte*, and the post-Kantian idealists, who in aiming for the absolute, took no notice of concrete human aggregates and their specific features, Cattaneo invited others to study the most diverse situations and to pay careful attention, not only to "repetitions and similarities", but also to the "variety of historical description".[36] Therefore, in his considerations on the principle of philosophy ("Considerazioni sul principio della filosofia"), he wrote that:

> [...] we will only have full knowledge [of man and his world], when we have carried out historical analysis of all histories, and clarified how the intelligence and will of the individual peoples is represented in each of them, whether the peoples concerned were left to the course of native traditions, or stirred to the alternative of mutual reactions, for in this way the history of peoples becomes the history of humanity.[37]

Despite reaffirming modern confidence in human progress in the light of his historical and anthropological reflections[38] against both the myth of the noble

---

[35] *SF*, I, pp. 102-3. If psychology is the study of the faculties and operations of the human mind, then ideology is the study of those ideas which human beings, living and engaging with others and with nature, produce in space and time and converge on the common wealth of humanity.

[36] *SF*, I, p. 155.

[37] *SF*, I, p. 151.

[38] One might think in this connection of the long series of writings he devoted to the world's most varied population, ranging from Great Britain to Sardinia, from India to Ireland, passing

savage and the superior state of nature argued for by Rousseau[39] and "Machiavelli's and Vico's wheel of fate" on the one hand,[40] and the "eternal dominion of evil" present "in Judaism and in Christianity" on the other,[41] Cattaneo highlighted the irregular course of human progress, comparing it to that of a river which is able to reverse the direction in which it flows at any time. Linked to a multiplicity of factors that can be documented historically and with precision, the life and movements of peoples are certainly affected but not determined by natural environment, because the natural environment is in turn shaped by its inhabitants through the "acts of intelligence", "labour", "efforts" and "works" which they carry out over time. "Where man is savage, the land is savage", he later wrote, in 1857.[42] Many years earlier Cattaneo had written of the Lombard lowlands and their transformation over the course of many centuries, expressing the idea through what he called an "artificial country":

> If we confine our attention to the narrow area between Milan, Lodi and Pavia, and look one by one at the attempts made to turn up the natural deposits and render them more receptive to the influence of sun and rain, it is easy to calculate that, in such a small area, the commercial value equal to several thousand million lire of work must be invested. This area's ability to feed a population, what might be called its natural or uncultivated fertility, would amount to perhaps one-tenth of that value. In other words, nine-tenths of the land is not the work of nature, it is the work of our hands, an artificial country.[43]

---

via Lombardy and China – ancient and modern – Japan, Mexico and Tunisia. But there is also an incalculable number of references to the populations of the past, more or less remote, as well as to contemporary groups through travellers' and explorers' accounts of their travels.

[39] Later on he would recognize, in the *Psychology of Associated Minds*, no less, that "Rousseau, generous, poor and without honour, praised the savage life only in order to shame an unequal and inhuman society" (see p. 92 in this vol.). In his inaugural address given in 1852, he had suggested that *Du contrat social* was one of the "two great philosophical initiations" (the other being Locke's critique of innate ideas) to the great changes that took place in the late eighteenth century (*SF*, II, p. 13).

[40] *EP*, IV, 504. On Machiavelli's and Vico's role in affirming a modern approach to the "facts of human society", similar to that applied by the physical sciences to nature, see *SSG*, II, p. 436. On these themes cf. Focher, (1987).

[41] *EP*, IV, p. 504.

[42] *SF*, I, p. 347, where Cattaneo seems to reverse the famous line by Tasso, "The land did like itself the people breed". (Translator's note: *Jerusalem Delivered*, I. 62, 5, trans. by Edward Fairfax.)

[43] *SE*, III, p. 5. For Cattaneo's *Notizie naturali e civili su la Lombardia* (*NNCL*), cf. the new edition, including substantial unpublished material, by Bigatti (2014).

But there are countless pages where Cattaneo dwells on the "acts of intelligence" and "works" performed in every part of the world by the different populations and passed on from generation to generation, along with all the other collective creations, norms, beliefs, labour techniques, and so forth, which make up their culture.

In considering the role of collective "ideas" in social dynamics and the process of civilization, Cattaneo would later adopt the concept of "system" as one way of making sense of human reality, and in due course would devote specific analysis to it, as we shall see shortly.[44] The tendency to organize ideas, he argued, is "second nature to our intellect" (even in man's savage state he makes "what he finds around him into a system"[45]), and as systems are developed in individuals through the relations which they have with their peers, starting with their mother, who is the first messenger of the culture of the "society" to which they belong, so too do systems of peoples develop through interactions between the cultural systems expressed at the various stages of their progress. It is in mutual exchanges that the various "ingrafts" are created, which then alter the existing "systems"[46] to generate new "historical combinations".[47] These in

---

[44] The first time he did so was in an article entitled "Frammenti di filosofia civile", published in *Il Crepuscolo* X. 10 (31 May 1859), 202-5. The second time was the second lecture included in the *Psychology of Associated Minds*, delivered to the members of the *Istituto Lombardo* in August 1860 and published in *AIL*, an abstract of which was published in *Il Politecnico* IX. L (August-September 1860), pp. 218-23 with the title "On the Formation of Systems".

[45] *SF*, I, p. 422.

[46] Referring to China, in 1861 he would write as follows: "The Chinese system, like all systems of ideas which did not come into close contact with other systems, was able to develop and spread; but it was not able to emancipate itself from *its principle*. Systems are like plants whose vegetation is always as it was when it first came forth from its seed; and is unable to change aspect save by means of an ingraft from another plant". And he added: "The fact that its principle remained did not preclude the Chinese system from developing in proportion to its *inventive* spirit: hence it continued to generate arts and studies on its own the whole time. Nor did it remove its *expansionist* spirit; hence it embraced, in China itself and the regions closest to it, a space which comprised four million miles and five hundred million men. [...] If anyone who considers China to be motionless consults the history books, they will see it has been stirring the whole time [...]; and this when Europe was stubbornly savage and impotent" (*SSG*, III, pp. 161-62). The same words are found in the Lugano school lessons on *Ideology* published in *SF*, III, pp. 96-97.

[47] In this connection he would later write as follows: "The historical combinations which result from the meeting of chance encounters and native traditions form as many different series as there are peoples, and all of them must make their own special conclusion to science" (*SSG*, II, p. 120). On the concept of "ingraft", cf. the preface to vol. II of *Alcuni scritti*, in *SSG*, II, pp. 109ff., where the inclination to usurp and oppress, which is only too present in "civilized" European peoples is equally criticized. Cf. also the conclusion to his essay "Sui disastri dell'Irlanda negli anni 1846 e 1847", in *SP*, IV, p. 21.

turn become ever more established systems, if other ingrafts from outside or other external drivers of change do not emerge. And when a system becomes rigid and closes, its dynamism and ability to change weakens, resulting in stagnation and decline.

The different paths taken historically by East and West speak volumes in this regard, as Cattaneo argues in the pages he devotes to the issue of growth and the factors that can obstruct or facilitate it. The oriental peoples led the way in terms of civilization, but eventually became closed into rigid systems based on the principle whereby the will and reason of the peoples reside "in the supreme ruler and his ministers", with the result that all subjects, more or less "resigned or indifferent to their fate", are obliged to wait for a sign from the monarch who is seen as the "father of the state", in the same way that the father is seen as "the king of the family".[48] In Europe, by contrast, the multitude of forces, powers, organized forms and ideal principles generated fierce battles, reinforcing the critical spirit and questioning absolute political power, dogmatic truths and the authority of tradition, making continuous innovation possible, with the result that "each successive generation can say it is almost a new people".[49]

This leads to two general assumptions which Cattaneo formulated in his "Considerazioni sul principio della filosofia" in 1844: *the more civilized a people, the greater the number of principles contained in it*; and *history is the eternal struggle between the different principles that aim to absorb and standardize the nation*.[50] At the same time, he added that these were the "foundations of a theory" that could be "expanded considerably", a clear allusion to liberal-democratic implications that Cattaneo was able to expound more explicitly in the new phase of his life, which began in 1848, the year of "portents" (referring to the European revolutions including the one in Italy).

Cattaneo to this point had pursued the line of civil progress and reform, but when the Milanese insurrection against Austrian domination broke out, he took an active part and became head of the Council of war that led to the city being liberated after five days' armed struggle.[51] However, the 1848 uprising resulted only in defeat, as in the first war of national independence. Once the

---

[48] SSG, III, pp. 136-37 and p. 141. Such closure was obviously always relative, given the characteristics of human nature, as is seen in the case of China. On Cattaneo and Asia, cf. Martirano, (2006, pp. 43-70).

[49] SF, I, p. 155. On the idea of Europe in Cattaneo, cf. Cofrancesco, (1981, pp. 31-5).

[50] SF, I, p. 157.

[51] On Cattaneo's participation in the events of 1848, see TO (pp. XVff.); and Della Peruta, (2001, pp. 61-77).

Austrians had returned to Milan, Cattaneo decided to set up home in Lugano, where the liberals, led by his childhood friend Stefano Franscini, were governing Canton Ticino.[52]

In Lugano he devoted himself to reconstructing events in Italy and to gathering documents to feed collective reflection.[53] He argued for federalism as "the theory of liberty" and peaceful coexistence, which could ensure the unity of the national order but also autonomy for the various internal regions, as well as peace and free progression among peoples at the European level, who had been continuously tormented by war and conflicts. Cattaneo also contributed to discussions on reforms in Ticino itself, putting forward concrete proposals for the development of education, for reclaiming the Magadino area, the construction of railways (cantonal and Alpine), in connection with which he argued for the construction of the Gotthard line as best suited to bringing the more developed part of Europe closer to the Mediterranean and from there to the Orient via Suez.

Having taken up a position teaching philosophy in the new cantonal high school, from 1852 Cattaneo began a new phase of reflection on the big issues that had concerned him to this point, with the intention of putting together "a new volume on philosophical subjects".[54] In a letter which he wrote in 1855 to his friend Cernuschi, who had been his right-hand man during the Milanese insurrection, he said he was happy to "have been forced by circumstances to return to studies from which his mind had been diverted", and to have "found", in constructing the outlines for his lessons, that there was still "new ground" to be ploughed.[55]

---

[52] On Franscini, with whom Cattaneo went on a journey to the Swiss confederation in his youth, see the collective volume edited by Agliati, (2007). On the Swiss period of Cattaneo's activity, see Fugazza, (1989), and Moos (1992).

[53] After Cattaneo had published a revised and expanded version of *L'insurrection de Milan* in Lugano (the original had been rushed by Cattaneo to Paris, where he had gone to drum up support for the Italian cause from republican France), he devoted himself to collecting documents on the 1846-48 period, of which he published three volumes between 1850 and 1855 (*Archivio triennale delle cose d'Italia dall'avvenimento di Pio IX all'abbandono di Venezia*). These three volumes have been republished in *TO*.

[54] *EP*, II, p. 330.

[55] *EP*, II, p. 350. It was G. Cantoni who soon after Cattaneo's death, was the first to draw attention to the originality of Cattaneo's philosophy course, (1870, pp. 13-16 and 1887, pp. 193-205). Cantoni was soon followed by Alberto Mario, who, in a letter to Bertani dated 14 January 1874 (kept in the Cattaneo archive and quoted by Bobbio in *SF*, I, p. LXII), wrote of lectures that should "all be printed" on account of the "treasures" contained in them.

In his inaugural address, Cattaneo emphasized the committed nature of philosophy, which in his view was not to "remain distant from the destinies of the people among whom it dwells", given the role it had as "thought which explores the nature of thought" and "brings together all rays of scientific light", in particular knowledge regarding "the world of peoples, the order of humanity, and the life of states". He dwelt on the social origin of ideas, affirming that, in order to shed light on the "individual intellect's efforts", it is necessary to investigate the "developments of adult and associated minds", namely languages, literatures, mythologies, laws, sciences and the other great expressions of humanity.

If his inaugural address spoke of "civil philosophy", the course did not fail to discuss issues of "natural philosophy" as well. Indeed, Cattaneo began with a lesson on *Cosmology*, that is, the study of man in *space*, *time* and *order*, again from a historical and cultural perspective, with the intention of illustrating the transition from the first representations of the universe to the most recent theories founded on the results of cutting-edge research:

> The primitive wise men had to struggle to fashion for themselves any kind of image of a world which for them was entirely unknown and inaccessible; and were able to describe man only insofar as he appeared to them in their private consciousness and in the practice of their life.
> While on the one hand modern philosophers are able to continually expand and adjust their notion of the *universe* by means of rigorous calculations and with the proof offered by instruments and operations, on the other they can represent *man* for themselves as he appears in the summary evidence of all times and all places.[56]

The second part of the course, on *Psychology*, sought to examine the mental activity of man as he has evolved over time, educating himself "to increasingly high levels of intelligence", to the point where he is able to "raise himself up and fly through the chasms of the universe" to the "immensities of time".[57] Cattaneo starts from "facts or phenomena" in order to shed light on human "faculties", instincts (in particular "the most powerful instincts of socialization and imitation"), sensations, memory, association, and imagination, moving on to reflection and "rational and deliberate volition". Through associations of minds and by accumulating combinations of ideas, men, in the course of their

---

[56] *SF*, II, p. 60.
[57] *SF*, II, p. 106, p. 87.

civilization, have "gone from the lowest levels of intelligence to the heights of scientific and inventive reasoning":

> But this does not happen to one man on his own, or to a society of just a few people or even one nation alone; but over the continuous succession of different periods of time, among many different nations, throughout all of humanity. Science is built not by the solitary mind but by *associated minds*, joined together.[58]

The third part of the course was concerned with *Ideology*, the study of how ideas "are formed" in individuals and in groups of people, of how they organize themselves around "principles" and form collective constructions.[59] Here Cattaneo dwelt on the role played by language in mental processes, and the dynamics of how "systems" of ideas built around principles that exercise such an influence on the way in which human beings think and act in society come to change.

In the next part, on *Logic*, the focus was on the "connection between ideas", and hence, for example, on the relationship between genus and species, or between "unity" and "diversity" which, according to Cattaneo, are issues of vital importance to the development of human knowledge, for if "we do not combine phenomena into unity, [...] all phenomena will remain unconnected", and if "we fail to distinguish phenomena in their variety, we will always see only being and never beings, [...] we effectively deny life itself".[60]

The final part of the course, on *Law*, *Ethics* and *Economics*, examined human action in the various spheres of social life: in the family, state, nation, religion, trade and humanity at large. As the law changes with social order ("as the idea of the social order in which man participates is played out in his conscience, so too is the idea of law"[61]), so too does ethics, which is the "internal regulator" of life that reflects changes in the law "in the individual's conscience".[62] It is in the process of civilization that human beings, by reflection, "reach the loftiest ideas",[63] become conscious of their shared human nature, and confer universal value upon rights by virtue of their ability to "raise themselves up", not just to the immensity of space and time, but also to the point

---

[58] *SF*, II, p. 127.

[59] *SF*, II, p. 9 and *SE*, III, p. 362.

[60] *SF*, III, p. 228. It is barely necessary to note that here we see Cattaneo's federalism in embryonic form.

[61] *SF*, III, p. 334.

[62] *SF*, III, p. 335 and p. 343.

[63] *SF*, II, p. 197.

where they formulate ethical and legal principles that can embrace "people of all groups and all religions":

> Out of the chaos of histories, ancient and modern, thus arises a *constant* and *universal truth*, a *law*; and it is the action of a moral force that emerges from the conscience when enlightened by a new idea, and drives people towards a single, *universal association*, which is the realization of *universal law*.
> The principle of this law resides in what man recognizes *in each of his peers*; what man recognizes *in himself is all men*; what man feels *in his ego is mankind*. [...]
> The *fact* of the equality of men, insofar as it is recognized by the conscience, is the foundation of the law and every subsequent version of it.[64]

Moving on to *Economics*, finally, Cattaneo clarifies that this discipline studies human activity as it is directed towards the achievement of utility ("right from his origins, among the multitude of objects surrounding him, he had to *seek out* rather those ones he had recognized as being *useful*, able, that is, to meet his needs, whether natural or human"[65]), highlighting the role of intelligence and will as the primary factors in individual and collective wealth, points he had already made repeatedly and would continue to make until the end of his life. It is intelligence, he writes here in his philosophy lessons, that is "the source of all progressive wealth", because intelligence "tends, through perpetual efforts, to procure an increased quantity of useful things for a given number of men, or the same quantity of profitable things for an increasing number of men".[66] If all men "continued along the paths of justice and equality", Cattaneo continued in his lectures, "each man would be able to devote himself to the work to which he is best suited and most inclined, and would be able to go about it with greater understanding and alacrity".[67] But where there are interests, abuses and privileges also emerge, with the result that wealth is created but not distributed fairly.[68] And since socio-cultural "systems" are capable of forcing "multitudes to follow more or less willingly the unyielding interests of the few",[69] it was up to "free reason", that is, critical thought, to reveal and tackle ethically unacceptable iniquity

---

[64] *SF*, III, pp. 340-41.
[65] *SF*, III, p. 407.
[66] *SF*, III, p. 409.
[67] *SF*, III, pp. 410-11.
[68] "Thus in various ways, the greatest fruit that men's growing intelligence enabled them to derive from their labours is shared unequally between them, based on titles that are more or less unjust depending on who holds them, who contributes some other labour or profitable function by way of compensation, and who takes the lion's share" (*SF*, III, p. 412).
[69] *SF*, I, p. 347.

and to translate "complaints" into wise ordinances to help the will position itself better and contribute to the building of "public" riches and "common" wealth.

As well as the lessons delivered in Lugano, parts of which were published only subsequently, during the 1850s Cattaneo also poured his historical and anthropological reflections into the pages of periodicals, writing reviews on stimulating publications, Thus, in reviewing the *Kalevala*, a collection of works of folklore and mythology by the ancient Finnic peoples, he drew attention to the obscure "origins of Europe",[70] and in presenting Longfellow's poetry he expressed his appreciation of literature inspired by the "dictates of humanity and justice".[71] And if, in introducing Francis Galton's *The Narrative of an Explorer in Tropical South Africa*, he appealed to scholars to study the most remote and unknown groups of people, in commenting on *The Formation and Progress of the Tiers État* by Augustin Thierry (having already reviewed his *History of the Conquest of England by the Normans* in *Il Politecnico*), he expressed his enthusiasm for the new European historiography, which had shifted attention from the upper reaches of society to the "more numerous and obscure classes",[72] and hence to their "organic and impersonal products", such as the "religion, language, laws and literature of a people".[73] A historiography, in other words, that was able to combine "thought" with "facts", interpretation with "the most rigorous discussion of documents",[74] which Cattaneo hoped would be adopted in Italy too, to address the big issues of national history. Similarly, after reading Giuseppe Ferrari's *Histoire des révolutions d'Italie ou Guelfes et Ghibelins*, published in 1858 in Paris, Cattaneo wrote his essay on the city as the "ideal principle" in Italian history (*La città considerata come principio ideale delle istorie italiane*), published in Carlo Tenca's *Il Crepuscolo*, reiterating his conviction that it was only with reference to the "ideal principle" of the city that it was possible to reconstruct "thirty centuries" of Italian

---

[70] Cattaneo saw such origins as being linked to the emigrations from Asia towards the west through three main areas, namely "the *Finnic*, the *Indopersian*, and the *Semitic*". On Cattaneo and European history, see Galasso, (2013, pp. 83-97).

[71] Cattaneo was such an admirer of Longfellow that he knew some of his poetry off by heart, as Jessie White Mario noted in their reminiscences published in *The Contemporary Review* (subsequently taken up in Alberto and Jessie Mario, *Carlo Cattaneo. Cenni e reminescenze*, Rome, 1884, p. 153), adding: "For him the *Slave's Dream* was 'the most graphic of modern poems'".

[72] *SSG*, II, p. 339.

[73] *SSG*, II, pp. 340-41.

[74] Unlike the ancient historians, who "used to speak on their own authority without indicating step by step how they had reached the conclusions they were recounting", Cattaneo observed, modern authors such as Ranke, Thierry, Thiers and Mignet had acquired the habit of documenting "which sources they had drawn on, and specifying what degree of reliance could be ascribed to them" (*SF*, III, p. 297 and *SSG*, III, p. 366).

civilization without getting lost "in the labyrinth of conquests, factions and civil wars, and in the relentless making and unmaking of states".[75]

The most representative of Cattaneo's writings on the subject of philosophy in the 1850s was certainly his "invitation to lovers of philosophy" ("Invito alli amatori della filosofia"), which was published in the *Rivista contemporanea* in 1857. Here Cattaneo offered a rapid and vibrant overview of the conceptual system he had developed and which underpinned all of his output in this area.[76] He underlines the two-way relationship between man and nature, and between the individual and society, in which the reciprocal chain of action and reaction is itself proof that the phenomenon is not a mere appearance but a force manifesting itself.

> Even our peers are phenomena as far as we are concerned; but active ones, which cannot help but have an effect on our conscience; whose action on us is as irrefutable and plain as that of our own ego is. Psychology and ideology struggle in vain to find the origin of all the individual's ideas in his *solitary mind*. Among the promptings and voices of his nursemaid, the infant progresses from blind instinct to his first confused sensations. From the most uncertain awakenings of experience, our mind wavers between the reciprocal impulses of associated minds. Other people's ideas interweave with our own from the outset: they awaken them, guide them, precede them, impose them. It is a rare mind that can boast of a single idea which has not come to him from others.[77]

Another essay written in 1857 comparing British and Italian agriculture ("L'agricoltura inglese paragonata alla nostra"),[78] which he wrote after reading a work by Léonce de Lavergne, became an opportunity for Cattaneo to show that in the light of history, all advancements in agriculture, from the most ancient to the most recent developments in English high farming, are no more than "*acts of intelligence*", and that the time had thus come to declare that thought is "a source of value *in itself*".[79] Two years later he published the first version of his

---

[75] *SSG*, II, pp. 383-84. Cattaneo had intended to write a review of Ferrari's work before responding to it with his essay on the *City*, as shown by the fragment, which can be dated to early 1858, found among his unpublished papers and published in *SPE*, III, pp. 296-98 (then in *SSG*, III, pp. 312-14). On Cattaneo's interpretation of Italian history, cf. Galasso, (2004, pp. 457-68); Castelnuovo Frigessi, (1975, pp. 265-82); Ingold, (2005, pp. 55-77); and Meldolesi, (2013).

[76] On Cattaneo's philosophy the writings of Norberto Bobbio (1971).

[77] *SF*, I, pp. 344-45.

[78] Cattaneo's friend Cantoni had given him this work, writing in a letter to Carlo Tenca dated 31 May 1857.

[79] *SE*, III, pp. 269-70.

work on intelligence as a source of public wealth ("Del pensiero come principio di pubblica ricchezza"), in which he argued more insistently that treatises of economics should include not only "nature, labour and capital" among the sources of production and wealth, but also "intelligence, which discovers the assets, invents the methods and instruments, and guides the nations on the road towards culture and progress", and "the will, which decides the action to be taken and faces the obstacles".[80] In other words, a "psychology of wealth" was required, and indeed the work published in 1859 bore the more general title "Fragments of Civil Philosophy". It is no coincidence that shortly afterwards, he published another work on "systems", an important concept for Cattaneo's reading of history and society, as we have seen.

While he was adding these new pieces to the jigsaw of his philosophy, the war of 1859, which accelerated the process of national unification, drove Cattaneo back to the role of journalist and cultural organizer once again, despite his decision to remain in Lugano where his philosophy teaching post ensured he could carry on making a living. First, he decided to relaunch *Il Politecnico*, which he had come to see as his own. Second, as he had done the first time in 1846-47, he republished a series of his own writings, on economics this time, under the title *Memorie di economia pubblica dal 1833 al 1860*.[81] Third, as member of the *Istituto lombardo di Scienze e Lettere*, he delivered the series of lectures which became the *Psychology of Associated Minds*, in which he outlined the main points of his philosophy.

Cattaneo's instructions to those who collaborated in *Il Politecnico*, old and new, were to deal with concrete issues of general interest, giving priority to the "scientific and cosmopolitan" dimension, and focusing in all cases on the dissemination of "ideas that are new, noble and free", because the point was to renew "our antiquated studies",[82] and to raise the cultural level of the Italian nation which was called to play an active role in a "living Europe" and to "show what it was capable of" in the areas of science, art and civilization.

---

[80] *SE*, III, p. 372.

[81] Of the planned two volumes only the first was actually published, by publisher and bookseller Francesco Sanvito in Milan in 1860. The first collection of Cattaneo's writings in three volumes was entitled *Alcuni scritti del dottor Carlo Cattaneo*. In collecting his writings, Cattaneo grouped them into four different sections: "Literature" and "Linguistics" (vol. I), "Fragments of Universal History" (vol. II), and "Civil Philosophy" (vol. III). Referring to the last of these three volumes, he said it was his intention to publish a fourth one as soon as possible, on "natural philosophy", and stated his desire to collect all his writings on the subject of public economy as well. On the fortunes of both editions see Lacaita, (2017, pp. 177-96).

[82] *EP*, IV, p. 167.

It was in this spirit that on 25 August 1859, he delivered the first of his lectures on psychology, entitled "Idea of a Psychology of the Sciences":

> Gentlemen, research into psychology is no vain grazing for idle minds. The psychological principle of *reciprocal sensory substitution* taught our forefathers an art unknown to the ancient world, provided a coherent education to those born blind, deaf or dumb. Now, there is in the nations an order of persons born blind, hundreds and hundreds of times more numerous, to whom the light of the truth is no light, – an order of persons born deaf and dumb, hundreds and hundreds of times more numerous, whose ears the voice of truth strikes in vain. But whereas in previous times the sciences were sworn to silence, mystically concealed from the uninitiated masses, now the spirit of the age requires them to be freely available to all peoples.[83]

For Cattaneo, to study the mind, its faculties and manifestations, to enquire into the "conditions" which had made scientific discoveries possible through the contributions of *"the associated faculties of several individuals and several nations"* (and which continued to do so),[84] meant to improve the action taken in order to help "the highest number" of human beings "to undertake all this additional mental activity that exceeds the limits of the lowest level of common sense".[85]

He also addressed the disparities between various people groups in terms of science and intellectual creativity. In his view such issues needed to be confronted with due rigour, first and foremost by applying the methodological principle of not drawing hasty conclusions based on partial observations and proceeding to cross-check the results with those obtained from other lines of enquiry. As he had already done with the seventeenth-century theories which had ascribed "the main influence in the genesis of civilizations" to climates, so too, in the face of contemporary doctrines which argued that scientific genius was a "distinctive of certain peoples",[86] or which attributed "a species of the human race to each different region", Cattaneo had no hesitation in criticizing such a deterministic approach, in the name of the truth demonstrated by historical observation, namely that many peoples that had previously been at the forefront of civilization had subsequently fallen into decay and extinction, whereas others had been barbarian for long periods of time, had subsequently joined the ranks of the most sophisticated populations. For Cattaneo this

---

[83] See p. 57 in this vol.
[84] See p. 61 in this vol.
[85] See p. 57 in this vol.
[86] See p. 57 in this vol.

meant acknowledging the fact that decadence and regression exist just as much as progress does,[87] which in turn begs the question: what is "this principle that infuses the spirit of life into the minds of the nations, and then suddenly abandons them to the slumber of death?".

Returning to the issue in the pages of *Il Politecnico*, in 1862 Cattaneo discussed the results of a particular strand of American anthropology, which, based on Samuel George Morton's anthropometry and the theory of the "plurality of types and their survival right from the primordial eras",[88] spoke of non-existent human "types", for example the Anglo-Saxons ("as imaginary in history and linguistics as it is in anatomy"), and in denying the "*common nature of nations*", went as far as to argue that the groups of people considered superior were entitled "to lord it over the earth and subdue or annihilate all other nations".[89] Against such tendencies, expressed in a book by two of Morton's followers, J. C. Nott and G. R. Gliddon, entitled *Types of Mankind, or Ethnological Researches* (Philadelphia-London, 1854), Cattaneo had no hesitation in denouncing a clear case of science being subjugated to political interests and degrading racial prejudice (Nott's and Gliddon's book also contained offensive diagrammatic representations of peoples of colour),[90] which deserved no more than to be stripped back to its "barbarian nudity" and rejected as a result.[91]

In contrast to opinions of this kind, Cattaneo summarized the concept of evolution, biological and cultural, which he had developed over the years, as follows:

We place man on the top rung of a ladder, which begins with organic monads and ascends to the savage, that is, the speaking creature. [...] And with the most animal-like savage there begins another scale, leading upward this time to the heroes of reason and humanity. Every nation that has produced one of these heroes is worthy of our admiration; but all the others are for us equally sacrosanct – we recognize no hegemonies over human beings.[92]

---

[87] See p. 59 in this vol.
[88] *SF*, I, p. 410.
[89] *SSG*, III, p. 243.
[90] *SSG*, III, p. 245.
[91] *SSG*, III, p. 243. On this issue see Fugazza (1989).
[92] *SSG*, III, p. 246. Elsewhere he stated: "The great chain of being has no interruptions. When the Cartesians tried to break it, they did so in vain" (*SF*, II, p. 134). It is also worth noting that while in 1860 *Il Politecnico* published one of the first Italian reviews of Charles Darwin's *Origins of the Species* (IX. 49, 110-12), Cattaneo soon developed a historical and evolutionist approach to the human world to complement that to the natural world. From his early years he had

Cattaneo ironically pointed out to those who boasted they belonged to a superior race they were in fact descended from groups of people who once upon a time were certainly barbarian, but who themselves had resolved, almost suddenly, "to pursue the new life of thought, and through the agency of dead and foreign languages, initiate themselves in the ways of those sciences that their very fathers had so despised".[93] This for him was excellent "proof that no part of the human race should even be despaired of, however entrenched in their primordial ignorance they may seem to be."[94]

Precisely one year after his first lecture, in August 1860, Cattaneo delivered the second chapter in his work on psychology to his colleagues at the *Istituto Lombardo*, "On the Formation of Systems", a key issue for Cattaneo as we have seen.[95] Pluralism and the degree of individual and collective liberty, indeed, the very ability of societies to keep themselves open and dynamic depends on the characteristics of their cultural, economic and political systems. The scientific model is once again the main example for him, its primarily quality being the fact that it is of benefit not only to "the material part of our existence", but also "in shaking up and renewing the systems", in keeping "our faculties in diligent tension".[96] Systems, he concluded, "must always keep themselves *open*; a finished, closed system becomes the graveyard of the intelligence and virtue which wove it together in the first place".[97]

The third lecture, "On antithesis as a method of social psychology", was delivered on 12 November 1863. After recalling the three fields of philosophy (philosophy of nature, the individual and society), and emphasizing the fecundity of the experimental method, which on the one hand had generated "family of entirely new sciences", and on the other, an increasingly vast and sure "field of philosophical generalities", Cattaneo underlined the importance again of the transition from an individual to a social perspective, which allows "everything that appears superhuman in the thought of the nations" to be

---

become familiar, through Gherardini and Rasori, with the theories of Erasmus Darwin, who like other early nineteenth-century naturalists such as Cuvier, Lamarck and Saint-Hilaire, discussed changes in the earth and living beings.

[93] See p. 61 in this vol. Elsewhere he had already been critical of every theory that "gratuitously assumes that certain races are naturally incapable of becoming civilized, and wraps the vows and efforts of unfortunate virtue in cruel and unjust condemnation" (ssg, I, p. 69).

[94] ssg, III, p. 244.

[95] See List of Texts p. 49 in this vol. for initial editions.

[96] See p. 78 in this vol.

[97] See p. 78 in this vol.

seen in a new light.[98] It is still necessary to continue enquiring "by what other means, apart from language, minds associated with each other in families, classes, peoples, mankind", can "work together with common intelligence, or against it; and how they came to operate with methods and results which for solitary minds would be impossible".[99] A central feature in the relations between associated minds for Cattaneo is the dialectic or conflict between them, which allows new ideas to be perceived and unknown truths to be discovered. If in the first lecture he had argued that "the electric current of thought needs a battery made up of many hearts and intellects",[100] here Cattaneo highlights, along with the various forms and degrees of opposition and contrast involved in the process of arriving at knowledge, just how productive the "conflict of several minds" can be, in every other field of life in association. "Antithesis", he wrote, "is not merely a method of scientific progress; it becomes a social principle in laws, governments and religions."[101] In the Lugano school lessons he had said that:

> Some antitheses last forever, such as the one between liberty and absolute power, the one between aristocracy and democracy, the one between philosophy or law and theology; the ones between the theologies of the different theological schools [...]. This continual war keeps minds alert and active; it forms the opportunity for new research and for new orders of ideas. Indeed, our adversaries' opposition [...] performs the same beneficial action in us as that of our teachers and correctors. The freedom of the press becomes useful to all opinions in this sense, of benefit even to those that hate it. Freedom of error is beneficial to the truth.[102]

The fourth lecture was delivered late in 1864, "On Sensation in Associated Minds", in which Cattaneo again emphasized the "social" nature of psychological activity, starting from the earliest sensations which each individual begins to perceive among the "associated beings" closest to them: their mother, whose "maternal instinct is associated with the instincts of the child", their family and other groups in the community. Like any other aspect of mental activity, including memory, imagination, reflection and judgement, sensation is linked to changes in society, in the sense that the more sophisticated society is, the more sensations grow, diversify and become linked with condi-

---

[98] See p. 78 in this vol.
[99] See p. 86 in this vol.
[100] See p. 62 in this vol.
[101] See p. 91 in this vol.
[102] *SF*, II, pp. 240-42.

tions and factors that are not merely natural but also social and cultural, such as musical, astronomical, chemical and electrical instruments, all of which are invented by intelligence. "Sensation in human beings is therefore not an unmediated encounter between the subject and various objects; it is not a *pure* fact; it is, right from its very beginnings, a *social* act".[103] And society does not merely "see" things, it also "does" them, with the help of the technology it uses, which increases the possibility of understanding the world with ever greater precision:

> Observers scattered in various stations who are exploring the earth's magnetic tension and the course of the winds and the rains are the parts of the civilized nations' *common sensorium*.
> [...] out of which, from a crowd of uncertain and occasionally contradictory sensations, a stable and serene light gradually emerges to represent the order of the universe.[104]

The last two lectures on psychology, delivered on 28 December 1865 and on 16 August 1866, were both devoted to "one of the great moral and material interests of human kind": "On Analysis as an Operation of Several Associated Minds". It is through analysis based on observable facts, for Cattaneo, that the scientific method has taken off in so many different directions. Neglected by "thinkers of an imaginative and fervid mind", and affected by "Brahminic, Buddhist, Eleatic, Platonic condemnation",[105] analysis is primarily the product of modern culture, and has established itself increasingly due to freedom of thought, which is obstructed by "closed systems" and the dominant interests of the "powerful", keen to impose "preordained" directions on it. For Cattaneo the primary duty of philosophers is therefore to fight to keep analysis free, plural, open and beneficial to all,[106] in the same way that it is the duty of enlightened legislators to facilitate the progress of knowledge through the increase of "special analysis".[107]

In this connection, at the end of the sixth lecture Cattaneo chose to resubmit the proposal he had published the first time in *Il Politecnico* in 1862, addressed to the Minister for Education Carlo Matteucci, who had sought his opinion on the issue of how to reform the Italian university system. In order to kick-start

---

[103] See p. 99 in this vol.
[104] See p. 102 in this vol.
[105] See p. 113 in this vol.
[106] See p. 110 in this vol.
[107] See p. 126 in this vol.

the analysis and make up for the delays that had been inherited from the past, Cattaneo suggested the government set up a network of "specialist chairs" at Italian universities, to go alongside the "general, standard chairs". These would be complemented by "free and innovative courses" given by young researchers, plus "*voluntary* lectures open to all" delivered by veteran teachers. In 1862 he wrote as follows:

> The principle required in Italian faculties is what in economics is known as the *division of labour* and what in psychology is referred to as *analysis*. The synthesis will be Italy. Synthesis is neither repetition nor uniformity; rather, it is the simplest expression of utmost variety. The more uniformity is eschewed, the fuller, or rather greater, your work will be, given that in such things there can never be completion or closure.[108]

By mobilizing cultural forces, the most important problems facing the country could be tackled in the light of the most up-to-date knowledge and with that clarity of ideas which he himself was seeking to attain in his contributions to the public debate. While he was publishing the lectures on *Psychology* along with various parts of the Lugano philosophy course (his inaugural address of 1852, and the three chapters on man in space, time and the natural order: *L'uomo nello spazio*, *L'uomo nel tempo* and *L'uomo nell'ordine*[109]), and while he was relaunching the issue of *thought as a principle of public economy*,[110] Cattaneo was publishing his writings on the main problems facing the nation in *Il Politecnico* and other journals of the period as well. These problems ranged from the infrastructure required to achieve proper unity and develop the country as a whole, to the school system at all degrees and levels, from the penal to the military system, to the administration of the unified state, to

---

[108] *SP*, III, pp. 114-15.

[109] As shown by the introduction, which despite its importance was never republished, Cattaneo intended to add another two chapters on man in *life* and man in *humanity*. See the short introduction (not published in *SF*, II) on man in the universe ("L'uomo nell'universo") in *Il Politecnico* (VIII. XLVI, April 1860, p. 345). Based on the lectures delivered by Cattaneo in 1862-63, G. Cantoni stated that "the subject matter for the fourth chapter, man in life, had been taken by him with supreme art from the results of the studies on the structure and functioning of the individual organs in living beings, both vegetable and animal". Regarding the fifth chapter on man in humanity, he stated that: "although vast and unduly arduous, it proved to be one of his finest and most fascinating, for he expounded his theme based on the data provided by ethnography, linguistics and ideology, all of which he had studied indepth" (1887, p. 8).

[110] The essay published in *Il Politecnico* has been translated into English: Cattaneo, (2003).

social issues and citizens' rights. These were all issues which Cattaneo continued to debate until his death, based on actual data and with one eye on the future, focused on the idea of a modern society, cultured, inclusive and supportive, able to make the "practice of freedom" effective for all, and therefore also more civil.

Introduction to this Edition

by *Barbara Boneschi*

The lectures: footprints on the sands of time

Jessie White Mario tells the story of how, when Carlo Cattaneo bid farewell to her and her husband Alberto Mario at Lugano in 1867, he did so in the following terms:

> "And now", said Cattaneo, as we parted, "I am going to be selfish – to shut myself up with philosophy, condense the studies of a lifetime, and leave some footprints on the sands of time". The quotation is his; he knew Longfellow by heart. For him the "Slave's Dream" was "the most graphic of modern poems".[1]

At the time, Cattaneo still nurtured the idea of compiling a work of philosophy that would bring together his life's research in this area, a project which, however, he was unable to complete in the time left to him.

The six academic lectures that Cattaneo delivered on the theme of the "psychology of associated minds" at the Istituto Lombardo between 1859 and 1866 would certainly have formed part of the work he had in mind. These lectures are the fruit of Cattaneo's mature reflection on this subject, and contain the theoretical nucleus of his social psychology. The lectures deal with the following individual subjects:

---

[1] Jessie White Mario, (1875, p. 482). Jessie White Mario (1832-1906); Alberto Mario (1825-83); Henry Wadsworth Longfellow (1807-82).

- Idea of a psychology of the sciences;
- On the formation of systems;
- On antithesis as a method of social psychology;
- On sensation in associated minds;
- On analysis as the operation of several associated minds, divided into two lectures.

They were delivered at the Istituto Lombardo, the scientific, literary and artistic academy founded in the time of the Cisalpine Republic. On 25 December 1810 it was renamed the Istituto Reale di Scienze Lettere ed Arti, finding its home in the Palazzo di Brera in Milan, in a room where the Institute's members still gather. After the fall of Napoleon, the Institute came under the control of government of Austria, and then, in 1859, that of Italy. Its name has undergone several changes over the years, but it is now known as the Istituto Lombardo Accademia di Scienze e Lettere.[2]

Cattaneo was admitted to membership of the Institute on 21 January 1843, and in the years that followed, received several important commissions.[3] In the aftermath of the five days' uprising in Milan, in which he was a leading figure, once the Austrians had returned, Cattaneo was forced to leave Lombardy in August 1848; he hurriedly sought refuge in Lugano (in Canton Ticino, Switzerland), which ended up becoming the permanent home for his exile.

In 1859, having been reinstated as a member of the Istituto Lombardo, he returned to Milan, given recently to the Kingdom of Sardinia, to deliver the first of these lectures; the second was delivered in 1860, then, following a hiatus in the years of 1861 and 1862, he delivered the next four from 1863 to 1866 at a rate of one per year.

His teaching of philosophy at the cantonal high school in Lugano covers the same period, albeit over a more extended timespan (from 1852 to 1865). These, then, were the years when Cattaneo's original thinking was turning in practice towards social psychology, the same subject he addressed in his Milanese lectures.

The relationship between lessons and lectures is clear from analysis of the manuscripts, which show traces of the former being used in the latter: the presence of the idea of "associated minds" as an appendix to

---

[2] Henceforth I shall refer to it either as Istituto Lombardo or as Istituto or by the abbreviation *IL*. The history of the *IL* fills the three volumes of the *ILASL*.

[3] On relations between Cattaneo and the *IL*, see Bolognesi, 2005, pp. 93-123.

his school lesson on "sensation"; his returning to the same subjects covered in the lessons, namely sensation and instinct, systems, antithesis and analysis, broadened to encompass a more social and historical perspective.

His predilection for the experimental method, which had proved to be such a productive and inexhaustible source of discoveries; the emphasis on scientific thought; and the social bond in the formation of thought, all dominant themes in the lectures, are present in the Lugano school lessons as well. For instance: "The building of science is the work not of the solitary mind, but of minds that are *associated* with each other";[4] or again, "To which is added the action of *society*, which operates on individuals with education, sympathy and force, first encouraging natural abilities and then discouraging them" (these considerations are expounded on in the psychology lesson on instinct).[5]

Cattaneo's psychology is concerned with mind and thought. One innovative feature of his studies is the fact that the moral link that joins or associates individuals is located not only in social aggregations or institutions, but also in the thinking part of the individuals themselves: "each mind entered into the course of thought already marked by the thought of others".[6]

In searching for an appropriate definition of the discipline he was developing, Cattaneo had thought of several titles: *On Associated Minds or Second Psychology; On Scientific Thought; Idea of a Psychology of the Sciences; Second Psychology or History of Associated Minds*, not in opposition to, so much as superimposed on, as he himself suggested, the *Psychology of the Solitary Mind*, or individual psychology or first psychology. He wavered between emphasizing the social dimension of thought or its scientific nature, but in his lectures to the Institute, there seems to be a preference for the title by which this portion of his civil philosophy has now come to be known.

It is possible to see the lectures as the point at which various strands of Cattaneo's vast erudition converge and take form to develop a theory of knowledge and thought deeply rooted in the fabric of society and the historical tradition. As Cattaneo himself had written several years previously, "it is obvious that the field of scientific enquiry is identical to that of history. It is obvious that science will not be complete, until we have examined all histories philosophically, and

---

[4] "Della psicologia in generale", *SF*, II, I, p. 127.
[5] "Dell'Instinto", *SF*, II, p. 135.
[6] Cf. sixth lecture on "Analysis".

clarified how the intelligence and will of the individual peoples positioned itself in each of them".[7]

Though Cattaneo's philosophy is incomplete, the lectures nonetheless are a work replete with important intuitions, profound reflections, and suggestions that find a surprising number of echoes and developments even in contemporary thought. This much has emerged from the various meetings held to coincide with the publication of the critical edition I curated. The first, promoted by AC-HII (A Colorni-Hirschmann International Institute), was held in Naples on 6 March 2017 with the title *Attualità della lezione cattaneana e le aree metropolitane di Napoli e Milano*; the second conference, entitled *Filosofia e Scienze umane. Modernità di Cattaneo*, took place at the Istituto Lombardo in Milan on 26 January 2017, the proceedings of which were published by the Institute itself in 2018; and finally, on 18 October 2017, *Un libro filosofico in corsa con il tempo. Il testamento incompiuto di Carlo Cattaneo*, a conference held at the Istituto della Enciclopedia Italiana.[8]

Notes to this Edition

The text in this volume is based on the critical edition of Carlo Cattaneo's philosophical lectures delivered to the Istituto Lombardo, which I curated, and which was published by the Istituto Lombardo (*PMA-EC*). My intention in *PMA-EC* was to reconstruct the lectures as an organic work. The text which resulted was the product of research carried out primarily at the Carlo Cattaneo archive and the Istituto Lombardo itself, both of which are in Milan.

My research indicated that as far as the philosophy lectures were concerned, both the number and date of which had previously been uncertain, a total of six were delivered in the period from 1859 to 1866, on the dates mentioned earlier. *PMA-EC* also contained the summaries of the lectures which Cattaneo himself compiled for publication in the Istituto Lombardo's *Atti* and *Rendiconti*; along with other versions or editions of them from the same period.

---

[7] *SF*, I, p. 150, "Considerazioni sul principio della filosofia", published in *Il Politecnico* VII. 39 (1844), 292-313, and republished with additions and amendments in *AS*, III, pp. 39-60, then again in *SF* (I, pp. 143-70).

[8] A video recording of the meeting, chaired by Biancamaria Frabotta with Tullio Gregory, Sergio Bucchi, Stefano Gensini, Carmela Morabito, Marina Piperno and Carlo Lacaita participating, can be seen on the Treccani Channel website on YouTube.

The present edition is based on *PMA-EC* but is more focused on the text of the lectures themselves. Two texts contained in *PMA-EC* have also been included as an appendix; the "Preface, 2nd draft", and the outline, or contents, "Psychology of Solitary Mind, Second Psychology or The History of Associated Minds"; both of which may be dated to 1855, and demonstrate Cattaneo's intention to compile a systematic work on the subject of minds in association which was never in fact completed. I have added my own notes to each of the lectures and two texts contained in the appendix, to provide further information, commentary and context.

Compared to the apparatus of *PMA-EC*, some footnotes have been removed, others added. Some of the footnotes contain references to others of Cattaneo's works, documenting the links with his Swiss philosophy lessons, the patterns underlying his interests and readings, and the wealth of knowledge he accumulated as thinker, writer, reviewer and teacher.

PMA-EC was a critical edition based on rigorous philological criteria, starting from the manuscripts and printed editions, with no attempt made to correct, normalize, standardize or modernize the text. Rather, I followed the manuscripts step by step, adding critical and philological apparatus to document the transcriptions and data to allow reference to be made to the original versions.

This edition is based on the same transcriptions as in *PMA-EC* but the following have been excluded from the previous edition: a) footnotes documenting variants or deletions; b) marginal annotations which provide no indication of where they are to be included and on their own are meaningless. I have also elected to omit a limited number of instances in the original texts where Cattaneo left ellipses or empty parentheses as a reminder to himself to insert sources, quotations or other references. By contrast, I have on two occasions included a full stop, and on one occasion the inverted commas closing a quotation, which were missing in the original, without drawing attention to this in footnotes, the reason being that the former were almost certainly mere oversight, and the latter quite possibly due to a different convention prevailing at Cattaneo's time. It goes without saying that Cattaneo's punctuation has not been followed absolutely in the English translation, which nonetheless has sought to be as respectful as possible of the author's choices.

The phrase "Cattaneo's note" indicates the three occasions on which Cattaneo himself added footnotes to his text. Every other footnote or parts of footnote not marked "Translator's note" or with any other indication of author are my own. The phrase "Translator's note" refers to instances where further information has been added for the benefit of the English-language reader, typically translations of phrases in other languages (Latin in particular; where possible existing translations, suitably documented, have been used). Square brackets display editorial interventions.

As in *PMA-EC*, underlinings in the manuscripts have been transcribed in italics.[9] The criteria adopted by Cattaneo were clearly not consistent in form or substance, hence no effort was made in *PMA-EC* to standardize such usage, and no effort has been made in this edition either.[10]

With reference to the titles of the individual lectures, lastly, the "List of Texts" shows the original titles, which contain a number of formal and stylistic inconsistencies, while in the rest of the work I have used only the simplified titles of the lectures, omitting sub-titled and additional specifications.

Acknowledgements

I should like to thank all those who have helped me in publishing this book. I am grateful in particular to Professor Carlo G. Lacaita, who encouraged me to do research on the texts that make up Cattaneo's *Psychology of Associated Minds*, for the care and attention with which he continued to supervise my work through to publication.

I would also like to express my thanks to the institutions in which Cattaneo's papers are kept: the Istituto Lombardo Accademia di Scienze e Lettere, the same institution where the lectures themselves were delivered; and the Civiche Raccolte Storiche of Milan City Council, which holds the majority of Cattaneo's manuscripts. Finally, I should like to thank the Comitato italo-svizzero

---

[9] Translator's note: The translation inevitably reflects the nature of the work as a critical edition, hence the preference has been for formal as well as dynamic equivalence. Clearly this decision affects graphic and textual features as well.

[10] Translator's note: In some cases this decision means that the conventions of standard English are not respected (for instance, certain book titles or foreign words are not in italics, to respect the original usage). Capitalization, by contrast, is one aspect in which the translation has sought to follow the rules of standard English usage. Also worth pointing out in this connection are the criteria adopted for the use of gender-inclusive language. While Cattaneo was clearly writing in a different period of history from our own, where possible in the translation efforts have been made to ensure that terminology whose intent was inclusive is inclusive in modern practice as well: hence "uomo" may be translated as "person" or "people", and so forth. Such usage is not absolute, however, and the reader is asked to bear this in mind.

per la pubblicazione delle opere di Carlo Cattaneo and the Comitato per il 150° anniversario della morte di Carlo Cattaneo, and the other institutions that have contributed financially to the publication of this volume.

I would like to thank the translator David Gibbons for the stimulating and insightful dialogue that has developed as a result of the initiative to publish Cattaneo's work in English. I thank the publisher for their kind and careful work.

Figure 1 Monument to Carlo Cattaneo, Milan, made by sculptor Ettore Ferrari.

Biography of Cattaneo's life

1801

Carlo Cattaneo was born on 15 June in Milan, which at the time was capital of the Cisalpine Republic. His father, Melchiorre, was a goldsmith, and his mother Maria Antonia Sangiorgi who had previously been widowed (her first husband's surname was Cighera). Carlo had four brothers and a sister. The family was educated but not well off, hence Carlo went to the Seminario di Arlenico above Lecco to study in 1810.

The Cisalpine Republic under French control became the Italian Republic from 1802 to 1805 and then the Kingdom of Italy from 1805 to 1814.

1814-17

In April 1814 the Austrian troops took possession of Milan, and in June Lombardy was annexed to the Habsburg Empire. In April 1815 the Kingdom of Lombardy-Venetia was established, governed by Francis I, Emperor of Austria and King of Lombardy-Venetia.

Carlo moved to the seminary in Monza in 1815, and continued with his studies; he supplemented his intellectual formation by visiting the library of one of his uncles on his father's side, and also that of his great-uncle Giacomo Antonio, who was parish priest at Casorate Primo in the province of Pavia.

In 1817 he came to study first at the Liceo Sant'Alessandro in Milan, then the Liceo di Porta Nuova. His teachers included the historian and man of letters Giambattista De Cristoforis, the grammarian Giovanni Gherardini, and the naturalist Enrico Acerbi. Carlo was a frequent visitor to the large libraries of Milan: the Biblioteca Ambrosiana, and the Gabinetto numismatico di Brera, conceived and directed by his cousin on his father's side Gaetano Cattaneo, which was housed in the historical Palazzo di Brera.

1818-20

The periodical *Il Conciliatore* was founded in Milan in 1818, but because of its liberal, romantic emphasis, was subject to interference from the censor's office, and shut down in 1819.

Carlo completed high school in 1820 and enrolled in the Faculty of Law at the University of Pavia, but failed to obtain a scholarship at Collegio Ghislieri. Thus it was that he began to attend the private law school run by the famous legal scholar and philosopher Gian Domenico Romagnosi, who had been lecturer at the University of Pavia and advisor to the government.

In December Carlo, still very young, began to teach the grammar course for the first years of the *Ginnasio municipale di Santa Marta* in Milan. Cattaneo devoted himself to teaching with exemplary commitment until 1835.

1821-24

Romagnosi was arrested by the Austrian government and taken to Venice, where he was imprisoned. In the trial that followed, where he was found not guilty due to lack of proof, Carlo Cattaneo stood as a witness for him. The secret police continued to be active in Milan targeting those suspected of conspiracy against the Austrians.

Late in 1821 Cattaneo departed for Switzerland for a journey with his friend Stefano Franscini, from Canton Ticino, who would subsequently become an educationalist, historian, statistician and liberal politician, involved in both local and federal institutions.

Cattaneo's first review article, "Assunto primo della scienza del diritto naturale di G. D. Romagnosi", was published in 1822 in the *Antologia*, a journal directed by Giovan Pietro Vieusseux.

He became friends with Giuseppe Montani, a man of letters from Cremona who would subsequently move to Florence and become editor of the *Antologia*. In these years Carlo was frequenting Milanese intellectual and business circles, members of the nobility, and the group that had formed around the poet Vincenzo Monti and his daughter Costanza Monti Perticari.

On 19 August 1824, he graduated in law from Pavia with a first-class degree, and continued teaching the first years of high school in Milan. He would continue frequenting Romagnosi until his death in 1835.

He duly obtained his diploma to teach letters and moved on to teaching the advanced course to the final years of the Ginnasio municipale di Santa Marta. He undertook studies and research on a vast array of subjects, learning German, English and French. At the request of the general director of high schools, Carlo Giuseppe Londonio, he translated several texts from German and revised a series of school text books.

1828-33

Cattaneo began writing for the *Annali universali di statistica (Annali)*, published by Francesco Lampato and directed by Romagnosi, an arrangement that would continue until 1838. In 1833 Cattaneo, who advised and worked closely with Lampato, published a series of articles, news items and reviews in the process; expanding and consolidating his knowledge and education as a journalist and disseminator of culture in the extensive branches of the natural and human sciences.

In 1833, publication began of the *Bollettino di notizie statistiche ed economiche italiane e straniere e delle più importanti invenzioni o scoperte, e progresso dell'industria e delle utili cognizioni* (the "Bulletin of Italian and international statistical and economic news and news of the most important inventions or discoveries, and progress of industry and useful knowledge"), part of the group of periodicals published by Lampato. The *Bollettino* was inspired by Cattaneo himself and it was predominantly him who edited it.

1835-36

On 8 June 1835 Romagnosi died in Milan, and was attended to by Cattaneo until his last moments.

On 19 October Carlo married in Trieste the Anglo-Irish noblewoman and native of Limerick Ann (Anna) Pyne Woodcock, the daughter of Ann Crosbie and Charles Brydges (or Bridges) Woodcock, whom he had met ten years earlier.

Ill health forced him to give up teaching in 1835.

Cattaneo was a scholar of society and economics, attentive to the transformations, innovations and discoveries attributable to industrial, technical and scientific modernity. In June he published an article on the project to build a railway from Milan to Venice ("Ricerche sul progetto di una strada di ferro da Milano a Venezia") in the *Annali*, to raise awareness and obtain support for initiatives to modernize the country. His activities as journalist and cultural advocate were complemented in the years that followed by those as consultant and businessman focused on achieving general economic progress.

In these years, with his friend, the philosopher Giuseppe Ferrari, he also began publishing the posthumous works of Romagnosi.

1837-38

Cattaneo published *Le ricerche economiche sulle Interdizioni imposte dalla legge civile agli israeliti* ("Economic research on the interdictions imposed by civil law on the Jews") with the date 1836, in which he argued for the abolition of discrimination against the Jews. He also wrote several articles for *L'Eco della Borsa*, founded by Michele Battaglia.

He assisted the banker Giovanni Battista Brambilla in the administrative and technical formalities required to obtain the concession to improve street lighting in the city of Milan, using gas produced from fossil fuels; subsequently he, Giovanni Battista and his brothers Giuseppe and Pietro, and various other partners set up a company to obtain a contract from the city Council to implement gas street lighting in Milan. The contract was eventually secured by another company represented by Jules Achille Guillard several years later, in 1843.

Construction of the Milan-Venice railway was approved, and Cattaneo, who had been appointed secretary for the Lombard section, argued for the importance of the line passing through the principal cities lying between the kingdom's two capitals.

He wrote an article on silk banks for the *Bollettino* entitled "Alcune ricerche sul progetto di un Monte delle sete", in which he criticized plans to set up a credit institution for the pursuit of private profit.

1839-40

Cattaneo acquired the rights to *Il Politecnico* from the chemist Father Ottavio Ferrario and from Giovan Battista Menini, who had been the first holders of the licence, and edited the periodical himself up to 1844. The first issue in January opened with a Preface by Cattaneo. The project required a vast amount of editorial work, into which Cattaneo threw himself with great energy and erudition; he directed the periodical and published a series of essays in it, in his own name and anonymously, on the most varied issues, drawing on his extensive knowledge and its practical applications.

In 1840 Carlo and Ann went to live in what is now Via Monte Napoleone 23. He was appointed by the Governor of Lombardy Franz von Hartig to translate reports on English prisons from English into Italian, and then to write an essay on prison reform. The essay, entitled "Di varie opere sulla riforma delle carceri", was published in *Il Politecnico*, vol. III.

1841-43

In these years Cattaneo published numerous essays in the periodical on subjects as varied as economics, linguistics, literature, political science and natural sciences; he also reviewed works published by non-Italian authors, and generally contributed to the dissemination of the finest progressive culture of the time. Among his many articles, reviews and essays, we may mention his work on Sardinia ("Di varie opere sulla Sardegna"); on navigation and irrigation in Lombardy ("Prospetto sulla navigazione interna delle province Lombarde con alcune notizie sulla loro irrigazione"); on historical Indo-European linguistics ("Principio istorico delle lingue indo-europee"); and on chemistry for non-chemists ("Varietà chimiche pei non Chimici").

On 21 January 1843 he was appointed member of the Istituto Lombardo di Scienze Lettere ed Arti, the scientific, literary and artistic academy founded by Napoleon which then came under Austrian control. Among other things, the Institute provided advice to the Lombard government on administrative and legislative issues, and in this capacity Cattaneo received a series of important commissions due to his vast knowledge and appetite for learning.

In an essay on Georg Friedrich List's "national economic system" ("Sistema nazionale d'Economia politica del dottor Federico List"), published in *Il Politecnico*, vol. VI, Cattaneo declared his adherence to economic liberalism.

1844-47

The sixth congress of Italian scientists was held at Brera in Milan on 1844. In conjunction with this event, Cattaneo published an introduction to the volume entitled *Notizie naturali e civili sulla Lombardia,* a collection of writings by illustrious scientists. The volume was conceived and edited by Cattaneo, and described the civilization and economy of Lombardy; he also contributed chapters on geographical data and water for domestic use.

Alongside his analysis of specific problems, Cattaneo continued to produce works of philosophical speculation: for example, in vol. VII of *Il Politecnico* (the final volume of the first series), he published an essay entitled "Considerazioni sul principio della filosofia". Thereafter the periodical changed printers, moving from Pirola to Giuseppe Chiusi.

In 1845 Cattaneo accepted a commission to serve as "spokesperson" of the Society for the Encouragement of Arts and Trades of Milan, chaired by the businessman Heinrich (or Enrico) Mylius. The Society, which was a private organization that operated under the protection of the viceroy and government control, was devoted to the dissemination of scientific and technical culture in its productive applications and to promoting industrialization in Lombardy. Cattaneo worked hard on behalf of the Society for three years.

He also collaborated with other periodicals during this time, such as the *Rivista europea*; his contributions to this journal included essays on the British

Indian empire ("Sull'Impero indo-britannico") and on India, ancient and modern ("Dell'India antica e moderna").

He collected some of his previously published essays in the first of three volumes under the title *Alcuni scritti del dottor Carlo Cattaneo* (the other two volumes followed in 1846-47).

In 1847 he was awarded the title of effective member of the Istituto Lombardo, giving him an annual income. The Institute appointed him as part of a commission to answer the enquiries made by the British government, regarding the possibility of applying Lombard models of agriculture to the situation in Ireland. Cattaneo's answers are contained in a series of letters addressed to the British deputy consul Robert Campbell which were read to his colleagues at the Institute and then published in the *Giornale dell'I.R. Istituto lombardo e Biblioteca italiana*, with the title: "D'alcune istituzioni agrarie dell'Alta Italia applicabili a sollievo dell'Irlanda" ("On certan agrarian institutions of Upper Italy applicable to the relief of Ireland").

Cattaneo met the English economist and politician Richard Cobden, who was visiting Italy.

1848

In January Cattaneo was called to form part of another Institute commission, promoted this time by the deputy governor Heinrich O'Donnel, to draw up a programme for the reform of teaching in Lombardy-Venetia. Cattaneo was responsible for compiling the report; to that point he had remained outside of revolutionary initiatives in the conviction that the growing demands of an increasingly informed and dynamic society would soon transform the political situation as well.

On 13 March, Vienna rose up against Habsburg absolutism, resulting in the downfall and exile from the capital of chancellor Metternich. The Milanese patriots seized the opportunity, and on 18 March the insurrection which came to be known as the *Five days of Milan* began. Cattaneo sided with the people of the city, heading up the Council of war which he himself formed on 20 March with Giulio Terzaghi, Giorgio Clerici and Enrico Cernuschi. The Council took the operational and strategic decisions which were responsible for the insurgent's victory after five days of battle, following their firm rejection of the armistice which the Austrians proposed time and again, and which the city's provisional government had been minded to accept. The contrast between the provisional government and the Council of war reflected the differences within the Risorgimento movement between, on the one hand, the moderates (supported by the Mazzinians, for whom the objectives of Italian unity and independence were uppermost) who were favourable to King Carlo Alberto's intervention, and, on the other, the federalist republicans who, inspired by Cattaneo, were opposed to any act of unconditional obeisance to the House of Savoy. Ultimately the moderate position prevailed, King Carlo Alberto declared war on Austria and on 26 March entered Milan. The war was unsuccessful however, and the King was forced to surrender, followed by the signing of the armistice between the Piedmontese and the Austrians. Carlo Alberto withdrew his troops to beyond the Ticino and handed back the city of Milan to Radetzky, who returned to Milan on 6 August.

In the first days of August Cattaneo tried again to organize some sort of resistance in the mountain regions, even meeting with Giuseppe Garibaldi in Bergamo, but the news of the war he received ultimately persuaded him and Ann to seek refuge in Lugano. A few days later, Carlo departed for Paris, having been deputed by the national insurrection committee to solicit French intervention. Upon his arrival, he found that the news of events in Italy that had reached Paris was largely misleading, so to correct them he wrote a pamphlet in French which he published there entitled *L'insurrection de Milan en 1848*.

He then returned to Switzerland, where he received permission to remain in Canton Ticino.

1849

The married couple set up home in Castagnola near Lugano, where they were to remain for the rest of their lives. An expanded version and Italian translation of the work published in Paris, *Dell'insurrezione di Milano nel 1848 e della successiva guerra*, was published in Lugano.

Cattaneo declined the offer made to him by Carlo Rusconi, foreign minister for the Roman Republic, to take up the position of minister of finance; the Republic, instituted following an internal revolt in the Papal State, was governed by a triumvirate consisting of Carlo Armellini, Giuseppe Mazzini and Aurelio Saffi. Many of the patriots who had taken part in the Five Days' uprising took part in the Roman Republic as well. However, the Republic, which was established on 9 February 1849, fell in July the same year as a result of the intervention by French troops.

In the same year Cattaneo came up with the project of collecting and publishing deeds, documents and essays on what he called the "the holy war of Italy". Agostino Bertani, a doctor, patriot, politician, close friend of Carlo and the Cattaneos' own physician, also participated in the project, and had the Lombard provisional government's documents sent to Locarno.

1850-55

The project to publish these documents, under the title *Archivio triennale delle cose d'Italia* ("Three-year archive of the history of Italy") became vast. Cattaneo published the first volume in Switzerland with the title *Preliminari dell'insurrezione di Milano riferiti al moto generale d'Italia* ("Preliminaries of the Milanese insurrection in connection with the general uprising in Italy"; 1850); the second and third volumes were published in 1851 and 1855 respectively.

Cattaneo contributed to the reform of senior school teaching in Canton Ticino as author of a project which set out the general guidelines, and when the cantonal high school of Lugano was set up, he took a position as teacher of philosophy. In November, at the school's opening ceremony, Cattaneo delivered his inaugural address. He continued teaching philosophy at the school until 1865. He contributed to initiatives promoted by Stefano Franscini for the liberal reform of Canton Ticino, which aimed to achieve technical, scientific, agricultural and industrial progress for the region. Some of these initiatives included the project to reclaim the Magadino and build local and transalpine railways. It was Cattaneo who advocated for the Gotthard railway line.

The British ambassador George Hamilton Seymour, a relative of Ann, held conversations with the Russian Tsar Nicholas I, while another representative of Ann's family, the French diplomatic and politician Anatole Brenier, carried out an exploratory mission to Italy, eventually becoming ambassador in Naples in late 1853-early 1854.

1856-58

To illustrate his position on the transalpine railway issue, Cattaneo published an article in the *Rivista contemporanea* on the Lukmanier and Gotthard passes ("Il Lucomagno e il Gottardo"), which opened the debate on this subject in the same journal with Luigi Torelli. Through the mediation of Giovanni Cantoni, in 1856 he began writing for Carlo Tenca's *Il Crepuscolo*. The aim of Tenca's review was to "illuminate the different aspects of our economic and civil existence"; and Cattaneo published some of his most incisive essays in this journal, including notably his "La città considerata come principio ideale delle istorie italiane" ("On the city as the ideal principle in Italian history"; 1858).

Cattaneo was granted honorary Swiss citizenship in 1858.

1859

The growing tension between Austria and the Kingdom of Sardinia resulted in the so-called second war of independence. The Austrians left Milan on 5 June, and shortly afterwards Napoleon III and Vittorio Emanuele II entered the city. The Villafranca Treaty was signed, with the Veneto left to Austria and Lombardy, with the exceptions of Mantua and Peschiera, ceded by Austria to France, which then handed it to Piedmont.

Cattaneo returned to Milan, and having been restored to his position as member of the Istituto Lombardo, held the first in his cycle of lectures on the *Psychology of Associated Minds* on 25 August, entitled "Idea of a Psychology of the Sciences". Thereafter he gave one philosophy lecture there each year except for 1861 and 1862, completing the cycle in 1866.

In August Cattaneo reached an agreement with publisher Gino Daelli to relaunch *Il Politecnico*, which he continued to direct until the end of 1862. For Cattaneo the second series was to remain faithful to the first; however, Daelli was not of the same opinion, hence the agreement ended, and while Cattaneo continued to publish some of his writings in the journal in the following years, he no longer thought of it as his own.

1860

Cattaneo published the first volume of his essays on public economy (*Memorie di economia publica dal 1833 al 1860*), the idea being to collect a significant portion of his intellectual output. The publisher's decision not to continue with the project meant the second volume in the series never appeared.

Political elections were held on 25 March, and Cattaneo was elected as member of parliament in the seats of Sarnico, Cremona and Milan; his preference was for the latter, and he took up his seat for the fifth constituency of Milan.

In the same year Cattaneo contributed a wealth of empassioned and constructive articles on issues concerning the new Italy to *Il Politecnico*, such as the railways, public education, the death penalty, how to improve conditions in Sardinia, and overhaul the state administration. Also in *Il Politecnico* (vol VIII), he published a series of three articles on cosmology: *L'uomo nell'universo. L'uomo nello spazio; L'uomo nel tempo; L'uomo nell'ordine* (man in space, time and the natural order). The intention was to add a further two essays on man in life and man in humanity, but the project remained uncompleted.

In September, having been invited to meet Garibaldi in Naples, following the successful completion of the Expedition of the Thousand, which, starting from Sicily, had liberated the south of Italy. Cattaneo stated that he was opposed to the south being immediately handed over to the Kingdom of Sardinia, and proposed an assembly of Italian states. During the month he spent in Naples he also concerned himself with projects to build railway lines in the southern regions.

1861

Having decided to remain in Lugano, he rejected the teaching post offered to him by the newly established *Accademia scientifico letteraria* of Milan. Indeed, he was never to return to live in the city. The Canton Ticino government gave him several commissions; the Council of State appointed him member of commission of experts to reform the tax law.

In Italy, the minister for public education Carlo Matteucci, a well-known scientist, asked Cattaneo for his opinion on the project to reform higher education in Italy; Cattaneo duly formulated a response which contained a series of interesting proposals.

He published his essay on thought as a principle of public economy in *Il Politecnico* ("Del pensiero come principio d'economia publica"), and continued to write articles and pamphlets in support of the Gotthard railway line.

1865-67

Cattaneo resigned from his position teaching philosophy at the high school in Lugano on 28 October, following a public disagreement with the president of the Canton Ticino Council of State Luigi Maria Pioda. The appeals of the local community and Cattaneo's students were to no avail.

On 28 December 1865 and 16 August 1866 respectively he delivered the fifth and sixth (and last) lectures in the cycle on the *Psychology of Associated Minds*.

In 1867 he was again appointed as member of parliament; Florence became the capital of the Kingdom in February 1865. Cattaneo got as far as the threshold of the parliament but did not set foot in it, for he had no intention of swearing an oath of loyalty to the monarchy. Cattaneo decided to address the electorate directly, in a series of nine letters to them ("Lettere agli Elettori") published in the *Gazzetta di Milano*. Jessie White Mario wrote that these lectures represented "a programme for the Liberals of the future; every subject of interest or utility to Italy is exhausted. We cannot regret that he did not take his seat; neither time nor opportunity would have been his to speak such courageous, practical, all-embracing words".

1869

Cattaneo died in Castagnola on 6 February, and was buried in the small cemetery there. Some months later his remains were moved to Milan, and many years later, in 1884, placed in the *famedio*, the building within the Cimitero Monumentale where dignitaries are laid to rest. Ann too, who had shared ideals, friendships and adversity with Carlo in the period of history in which he played such a leading role, died in 1869.

Figure 2 Assembly Room of Istituto Lombardo, Milan, Palazzo di Brera (Sketch).

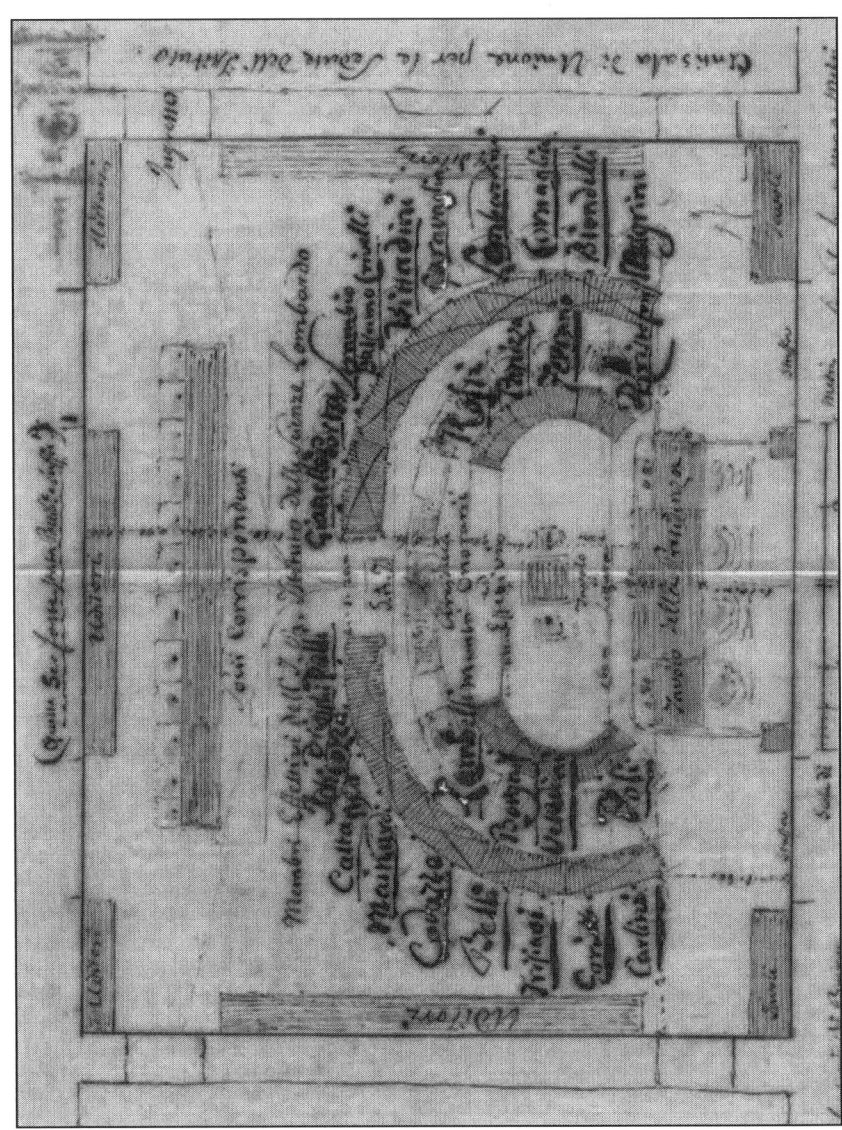

Copyright Comune di Milano – all rights reserved – Milano, Palazzo Moriggia | Museo del Risorgimento

List of Texts

This list provides details of the various manuscripts' locations in the archives and the publishing history of the texts themselves, both their first publications and their subsequent inclusion in the most important anthologies of Cattaneo's writings (OEI, SF and OPS).

1. Idea of a psychology of the sciences. Lecture I, 25 August 1859.

    The manuscript, which bears the title "*Idea d'una Psicologia delle Scienze*" ("Idea of a Psychology of the Sciences"), undated, is located in ACM, cart. 15, pl. III.

    It was first published in OEI, VI, 1892, pp. 261-74; this text was then checked, revised and corrected by Bobbio in SF, I, 1960, pp. 407-21. The abstract was published in ATTI IL, I, 1860, pp. 447-49.

    It is included here in the transcription I made of it in PMA-EC (2016).

2. On the formation of systems. Lecture II, 23 August 1860.

    The manuscript of the lecture is located in ACM, cart. 15, pl. III, bearing the title "Psicologia sociale. *Della formazione dei sistemi*" ("Social psychology: *On the formation of systems*"), undated but datable to 1860.

    This lecture was first published in OEI, VI, 1892, pp. 299-310; then in SF, I, 1960, pp. 421-33, including Bobbio's revisions.

    Previously an abstract of the lecture had been published in ATTI IL, II, 1860-61, pp. 133-36, and again in *Il Politecnico* with the title "Della formazione dei sistemi. Estratto d'una lettura fatta all'Istituto delle Scienze, del Dott. Carlo Cattaneo il 23 agosto 1860" ("On the Formation of Systems. Abstract of a lecture delivered to the Institute of Sciences, by Dr Carlo Cattaneo", 23 August 1860"), IX, August-September 1860, 50-[51], pp. 218-23.

    The subject was also discussed by Cattaneo in his unsigned article on "Frammenti di filosofia civile, (1852-1859) – I sistemi", in *Il Crepuscolo*, 31 May 1859, X. 10, pp. 202-5.

    The text of the lecture here is based on my transcription in PMA-EC, 2016.

3. On Antithesis as a Method of Social Psychology. Lecture III, 12 November 1863.

In *ACM*, cart. 15, pl. III; the full manuscript has not been found, only fragments.

The first publications of this lecture were as follows:

1) *Essay* in *ATTI IL*, III, 1862-1863, pp. 450-454;

2) *Dell'Antitesi come metodo di psicologia sociale. Lettura del D.r Carlo Cattaneo all'Istituto di Scienze e Lettere in Milano nell'adunanza del 12 novembre 1863* (Lugano: Veladini, 1864);

3) Untitled, on the front page of *Il Diritto. Giornale della democrazia italiana*, 24 December 1863;

4) "Dell'antitesi come metodo di psicologia sociale; lettura del dott. Carlo Cattaneo al R. Istituto lombardo" ("On Antithesis as a Method of Social Psychology; Lecture by Dr Carlo Cattaneo to the Royal Istituto Lombardo"), *Il Politecnico* XX. 92-93, February 1864, 262-70.

The text published in *Il Politecnico* was republished in *OEI*, VI, 1892, pp. 311-23, and in *SF*, I, 1960, pp. 433-46, with barely a handful of variants between the two versions.

The text here, as in *PMA-EC* (2016), is that of the pamphlet published in Lugano in 1864.

4. On Sensation. Fragment of a Psychology of Associated Minds. Lecture IV, 15 December 1864.

The manuscript entitled "Lettura all'Istituto Della *Sensazione* Frammento d'una *Psicologia delle Menti associate*" ("Lecture to the Institute On *Sensation* Fragment of a *Psychology of associated Minds*") is found in *ACM*, cart. 15, pl. I. The title suggests this could be the text of the lecture, for which the date would be 1864. This is the text used here, based on the transcription made in *PMA-EC* (2016), but was not the text published in either *OEI* or *SF*. *ACM*, cart. 15, pl. I also contains the manuscript of the abstract (*Estratto della Lettura fatta all'Istituto,* 15 Dec.[ember] 1864", published in *Rendiconti IL*, I, 1864, pp. 182-85.

In *OEI*, VII, 1892, the lecture "On Sensation in Associated Minds" was included as an "Appendix" to "Sensation", the Swiss psychology lesson (pp. 134-38); Bobbio in his edition moved the appendix "On Sensation in Associated Minds" and included it in the group of lectures on the *Psychology of Associated Minds* (*SF*, I, 1960, pp. 446-50).

The abstract published in *Rendiconti IL* and the versions included in *OEI* and *SF* differ only minimally from each other and also from the manuscript version of the abstract published in the *Rendiconti*.

5. On Analysis in Associated Minds, part I, Lecture V, 28 December 1865.

A manuscript bearing the title "Dell'analisi nelle menti associate. Seconda redaz.[ione]" ("On Analysis in Associated Minds. Second draft") is held in *ACM*, cart. 15, pl. III, undated but datable to 1865, which contains the lecture on analysis part I; I transcribed this text and published it in *PMA-EC*, 2016. This is the text used here.

6. On Analysis in Associated Minds, part II, Lecture VI, 16 August 1866.

A manuscript bearing the title "Dell'analisi nelle menti associate. 2. parte" ("On Analysis in Associated Minds. Part 2") is held in ACM, cart. 15, pl. III, undated but datable to 1866.

This is the text published in OEI, VI, 1892, pp. 274-98; and again in SF, I, 1960, pp. 451-79, the latter by Bobbio, which included his revisions. This is the same text I transcribed from the manuscript and published in PMA-EC (2016).

An abstract was published in RENDICONTI IL, III, 1866, pp. 213-15; there is no manuscript version of the abstract.

7. Psychology of Associated Minds. Preface. 2nd draft [1855].

The manuscript, whose title is as above, undated but datable to 1855, is found in ACM, cart. 15, pl. III.

The first full publication was by Fugazza in "Filosofia e scienze umane: intorno ad alcuni autografi di Cattaneo" (in *Cattaneo, Milano e la Lombardia, Incontro di studio n. 28, Milano, 29-30 novembre 2001* (Milan: Istituto Lombardo, Accademia di Scienze e Lettere, 2005, pp. 228-38). Here the text used is based on my transcription in PMA-EC, 2016.

8. Psychology of the Solitary Mind, Second Psychology or the History of Associated Minds. Outline or Contents [1855].

The manuscript, whose title is as above, is held in ACM, cart. 15, pl. III, undated but datable to 1855.

It was first published by F.U. Saffiotti in "Sulla legittimità di una psicologia delle menti associate", in *Atti del IV Congresso internazionale di filosofia*, 1911 (Genoa: Formiggini, undated), III. 640-6. Here the text used is based on my transcription in PMA-EC (2016).

Figure 3 Idea of a Psychology of the Sciences, manuscript's first page.

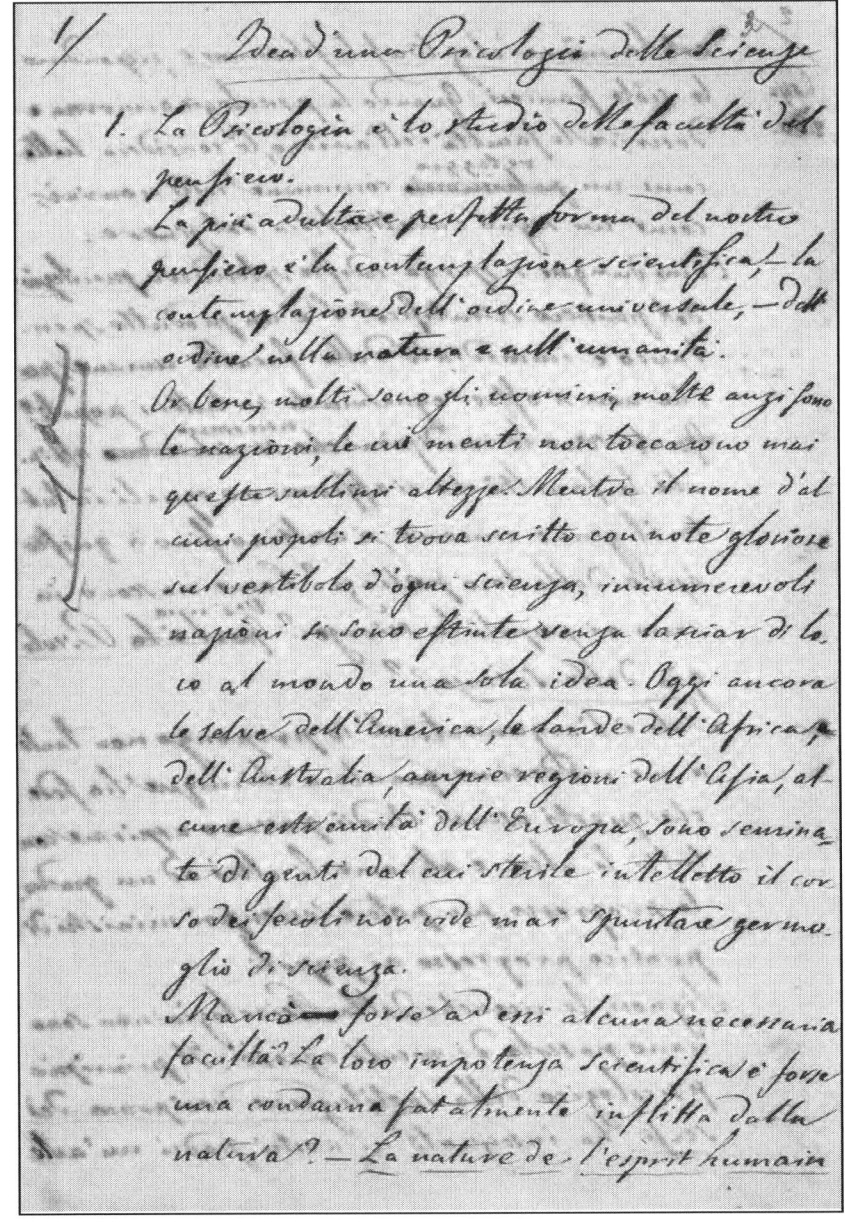

Copyright Comune di Milano – all rights reserved – Milano, Palazzo Moriggia | Museo del Risorgimento

LECTURE I
Idea of a Psychology of the Sciences

Notes

This is the first of the lectures on philosophical subjects that Cattaneo delivered to the Istituto Lombardo. Cattaneo, who had only recently been re-established as an ordinary member of the Istituto, proposed the following topic for his lecture, writing from Lugano on 16 August 1859, referring both to his Swiss philosophy lessons and another article previously written by him.

> It would give me pleasure to furnish you with an account of the research in which the opportunities I have had here have permitted me to engage. Thus I should like, if you will allow me, to read out a *paper* that I can adjust to the time – presumably brief – you intend to grant me. It refers to another article I published just over two years ago, in the *Rivista Contemporanea* of Turin; and its title will be *Idea of a Psychology of the Sciences*.[1]

The publication Cattaneo is referring to here is "Un invito alli amatori della filosofia".[2] Cattaneo's reflections in this period had extended to include the

---

[1] *EP*, III, p. 186, letter dated 16 August 1859; the original is found in *AIL*, papers of the Chairman and Deputy Chairman, despatch no. 513, dated 20 August 1859.

[2] "Un invito alli amatori della filosofia", in *SF*, I, pp. 339-57 (*Rivista Contemporanea*, Turin, May 1857, V, vol. X, XLIII, pp. 81-94, and subsequently republished in other editions). Bobbio describes this article as "the finest and most vibrant of his essays on philosophy" (1971, p. 96); for Momigliano (1920, p. 185), it "summarizes the ideas expressed in various of his philosophical writings over the course of two decades"; Saffiotti (1908, p. 314) commended the link which Cattaneo himself established between the first lecture and the earlier article referred to, seeing it as confirmation of "a peculiar characteristic of the thought of C.[attaneo], namely its systematic nature"; Saffiotti's article is in response to Gentile (1908, pp. 105-24).

means and method by which scientific knowledge is obtained, and how such knowledge relates to individual and social psychology.

A great sense of anticipation had been building for Cattaneo's return to Milan. The day was 25 August 1859, the date on which the assembly acknowledged the royal decree by which Alessandro Manzoni was made lifelong President of the Institute;[3] numerous and illustrious ordinary and honorary members were present, although not Manzoni himself. News of the event may be found in the *Gazzetta di Milano*, which gave an account the following day (26 August):

> Yesterday the royal *Istituto Lombardo di scienze, lettere ed arti* held the last of its assemblies for the year, and the first under its new Presidency. The hope that Alessandro Manzoni, unanimously elected as Honorary President, might be present; the news that Dr Carlo Cattaneo, elected secretary by a majority of the academic body, but then replaced by someone else for reasons unknown to us, was to deliver a speech, meant that there was quite a throng at this ceremonial scientific event. Manzoni did not attend, but Dr Cattaneo, who was most eagerly anticipated, did not disappoint, reading aloud a speech he had written on the psychology of the sciences. We hope that the enthusiastic welcome which the members of the *Istituto* and indeed the whole audience gave him will have convinced our illustrious fellow citizen of Milan that after ten years of exile, he might once again take up residence in our city, and so repeat those splendid displays of learning and intelligence that attracted universal attention for him in the Lombard capital.[4]

Cattaneo was "welcomed with expressions of great rejoicing, after an absence of ten years, by the academic body and the numerous persons who had come to hear him", we read in the Istituto's *Proceedings*; the minutes of the meeting state his lecture was "part of a much longer work, to be published in the academic body's publications".

---

[3] Alessandro Manzoni (1785-1873).

[4] The press response was enthusiastic; *Il Pungolo*, directed by Leone Fortis, wrote: "Our celebrated philosopher cum journalist read an essay to the Istituto on the Psychology of Science, bold concepts for which the new Prometheus stole a spark from the Sun to give life to their clay, in which he gave a soul to what so far had only had a mind" (27 August 1859); *Il Progresso* on the same date quoted a long article from *L'Italie*, written in response to more guarded comments in another newspaper, *La Gente latina*: "L'Italie holds Cattaneo in high esteem, respecting him for his decision to continue his exile in Lugano, and concludes that "the civil philosophy taught by him from his free chair in Lugano is a seed that will bear the fruits of progress to the benefit of our children as well; while good principles may be sown in one country, they are not destined to sprout in that one alone'".

Cattaneo's own impressions are described in a letter to the patriot Enrico Cernuschi,[5] one of the leading figures in the Five Days' uprising in Milan and the Roman Republic, who moved to Paris and became a financier, economist, and devotee and collector of oriental art, and was linked to Cattaneo through ties of deep friendship and shared federalist convictions:

> I should tell you that on 25 August, I went to the last of the Institute's annual assemblies, my invitations to which had been continued by the new President appointed by the new government. In expressing my intention to formally take up my seat, I had said that I would read a new paper. I found the room filled with friends and others who greeted me cordially, and was applauded at the start and end of my lecture. All the newspapers devoted more or less generous articles to me; but I was very reserved and quietly minded my own business. I found Milan rather like it tends to be in Mardi Gras week, full of people and in particular immigrants from the Veneto; the petit bourgeois restored and happy; the French numerous, popular with the families; few Piedmontese, stiffly keeping themselves to themselves; the volunteers' resentment towards them is great; the supporters of the Piedmontese are dissatisfied, except for the nobles who to me looked like *glory-hunting pricks*. But all classes seemed to have given each other their word and to have *conspired* to appear happy and harmonious. It is a *demonstration* to the diplomacy of Europe. The principle of all this politics is not *conscience* but *theatre*.[6]

The lecture did not disappoint the audience's high expectations: Rambaldi saw in it "the legacies of Romagnosi, the *idéologues* and the Enlightenment, combined to form an original vision enriched with nineteenth-century historicism, and open to positivist, romantic and idealistic suggestions."[7]

---

[5] Enrico Cernuschi (1821-96).
[6] *EP*, III, p. 208, letter dated 14 October 1859, to Cernuschi (*ACM*, cart. 2, pl. XIX, a. 1859).
[7] Rambaldi (2009, p. 361).

Idea of a Psychology of the Sciences

1. Psychology is the study of the faculties of thought.

The most adult and perfect form of human thought is scientific contemplation, – contemplation of the universal order, – of the order in nature and humanity.

Now, many are the men, indeed, many are the nations, whose minds have never reached such sublime heights. Whereas the names of some people are written gloriously in the halls of every science, countless nations have gone into extinction without leaving even an idea of them to the world. Even today, the forests of America, the scrublands of Africa and Australia, broad swathes of Asia, and some of the farthest-flung reaches of Europe, are scattered with peoples whose sterile intellects have never, in the course of the centuries, seen even a single scientific bud spring forth.

Were they perhaps lacking in some necessary faculty? Is their scientific impotence maybe some kind of condemnation handed down to them implacably by nature? – *La nature de l'esprit humain est la même chez tous les hommes*, the French school of thought replies. When psychology ranks and describes the faculties of the mind, it considers them all part of the shared legacy of all people, a characteristic of humankind.

How, then, should this splendid *privilege* of scientific thought be explained? If it is the spontaneous and immediate product of the human faculties, why does it not offer itself equally to all peoples? What are the necessary conditions for the faculties held to be equal throughout the human race in order for them to reach this pinnacle of their abilities? How are the sciences born among different peoples? Is there a *Psychology of the sciences*?

This is the subject I commend, not so much to myself, as to anyone who has faith that these obscure studies may aspire, with all the others and like others, to advance gradually to the point where they are able to administer practical progress to the peoples themselves.

Gentlemen, research into psychology is no vain grazing for idle minds. The psychological principle of *reciprocal sensory substitution* taught our forefathers an art unknown to the ancient world, taught a reasonable education to those born blind, deaf or dumb. Now, there is in the nations an order of persons born blind, hundreds and hundreds of times more numerous, to whom the light of the truth is no light, – an order of persons born deaf and dumb, hundreds and hundreds of times more numerous, whose ears the voice of truth strikes in vain. But whereas in previous times the sciences were sworn to silence, mystically concealed from the uninitiated masses, now the spirit of the age requires them to be freely available to all peoples. Those who disseminate the sciences must therefore investigate by which ways the highest number of minds can be stimulated and helped to undertake all this additional mental activity that exceeds the limits of the lowest level of common sense.

2. It seems evident to me above all that the issues entailed by the question are to be sought in human nature and not in the external and material conditions of the peoples.

In the previous century, on the authority of Montesquieu and Herder[8] primarily, the main influence in the genesis of civilizations and hence also of learning was attributed to climate. But there is too much evidence to the contrary in the history of the sciences for this. If India gave us decimal numbers, if and the Arabs gave us the concept or at very least the names of algebra and chemistry; the logarithm was invented in distant Scotland;[9] Newton, interpreter of the laws of the stars, lived in the foggiest of climates; and Linnaeus, who brought the whole vegetable kingdom together in the idea of the flower, lived among the snows of Sweden.[10] Quite irrespective of climate!

More acceptable, even in our day, is the theory that scientific genius is a distinctive of certain peoples. It is clear that each people tends to congratulate itself in thinking this. It is a form of what Vico described as *the conceit of the nations*.[11]

This natural and ancient hypothesis of *chosen peoples* has gained fresh force from the two new sciences that have arisen following the application of botany and zoology to geography. In the same way that distinct flora and fauna are assigned to each region of the globe and as certain species, indigenous to

---

[8] Charles Louis de Secondat de La Brède e de Montesquieu (1689-1755). Johann Gottfried von Herder (1744-1803).
[9] John Napier of Merchiston (1550-1617).
[10] Carl von Linné, or Linnaeus (1707-78).
[11] On Cattaneo's continuing interest in Vico (1668-1744), cf. Francioni (2018, pp. 13-24).

one region, represent other species of the same genus denied to that region and bestowed upon another, so too, as a complement to such great variety in creation, a more audacious theory attributes a species of the human race to each different region at the origin. Certain varieties, or mixtures of several varieties, according to this view are more physically or intellectually capable and better suited to forceful expansion over the earth by waging destruction or breeding with each other, obliterating the other primitive peoples in the process. Thus, those peoples become established that alone can be designated with the name of thinking species: *Homo sapiens.*

Gentlemen, my subject here is neither to accept this hypothesis nor refute it. Accordingly, it is beyond my remit to say how such odious inferences as appear inescapably to arise under this hypothesis to the detriment of weaker peoples, to the comfort of the consciences of every type of conqueror and oppressor, could be avoided. The conclusions that the supporters of the African slave trade drew from the discovery of a constant difference between blacks and whites in terms of *facial angle*, are well known: conclusions whereby they were able to argue that this people was incapable of lofty thought, predestined to vegetate in perpetual infancy, and required the protection of its enemies.[12] You see, gentlemen, if the hypothesis were proved correct, the iniquity of the consequences would not exonerate us from the duty of accepting disagreeable truths.

I should rather avoid this subject in our discussion altogether. Instead, I would prefer to point out that, while this theory enables the issue of the primitive intellectual disparity between peoples to be dealt with relatively easily, it still leaves unanswered the question of how a noble and wise lineage, which displayed its glorious learning for many centuries, could suddenly fall back into the most profound mental impotence. It would not explain how the Greek people, which previously had been so rich in every kind of intellectual fruit, for more than a thousand years did little more than provide shade to the land

---

[12] Cf. "Tipi del genere umano", in SSG, III, pp. 214-47 (*Il Politecnico* XIV. LXXXV (1862), 336-57), where Cattaneo describes the research on comparative anatomy carried out by Samuel George Morton (1799-1851). Morton, according to Cattaneo, "analysed in particular these differences between peoples, a field of study that had already been founded with the discovery of Camper's theory of facial angle. He sought to combine the study of human anatomy with that of paleontology, thus shedding light on the first steps of man, from his earliest appearance in the separate parts of the globe" (p. 216). The naturalist Georg (Giorgio) Jan (1791-1866), in an article entitled "Dell'uomo considerato come un proprio regno dell'istoria naturale. Prelezione al secondo corso annuo del prof. Giorgio Jan, part II" (published in Il Politecnico VI. 32 (1843), p. 141), had previously illustrated the measurements of degrees of prognathism carried out by Dutch naturalist Petrus Camper (1722-89). On this issue see Fugazza (2015, pp. 329-36, and 2018, pp. 67-69), who illustrates Cattaneo's position in the nineteenth-century debate.

of Constantine, as though it were no more than some kind of barren tree. It was not the sword of the Turks that cut down the intellectual life of Greece in the fifteenth century; it had been growing barren for more than a thousand years previously. Nor was it theological controversies, as some have proposed, that preoccupied people's minds and so shut them off from all other forms of thought. For as you know, the new life of Western thought was already stirring in the midst of the theological disputes at the Sorbonne in those same centuries. Today, we see five hundred million men, one-half of all mankind, belonging to inventive nations brought up in traditions of learning significantly earlier than our own, languishing as though intellectually petrified, like sediments of fossils bearing witness to a life that is no longer.

Unfortunately, by virtue of causes that undoubtedly reside in the domain of psychology, a people whose thought once illuminated the world for several generations is able to arrive at a generation that ceases to think, that all but buries the faculties that had borne so much fruit among its fathers, that even loses the awareness that it possesses such faculties, repudiating every new thought, every new deployment of its faculties, as though grounds for censure. Amid the rivalries of progress, gentlemen, science must not forget the painful lesson of decadence and regression, which too is a reality, which occurs, and which may bring about not only the lengthy decay of the peoples concerned, but even, on some occasions, their extinction. Is it the case, then, that an entire lineage is born without the intellectual endowment that so distinguished its fathers? And if it does have the same natural capabilities and fails to avail itself of them, what principle is it that so suddenly comes to be lacking in them? What is this principle that infuses the spirit of life into the minds of the nations, and then suddenly abandons them to the slumber of death?

Equally, the theory of racial disparity can no more explain how peoples that for so long were barbarian, such as the Scandinavians, Germans, Slavs and Magyars, could suddenly resolve – while southern Europe, which in the meantime too had returned to barbarous ways, could not communicate a scientific impulse to them which it no longer had – to pursue the new life of thought, and through the agency of dead and foreign languages, initiate themselves in the ways of those sciences that their very fathers had so despised. To solve the problem of the sudden transition of the primitive savages from wild nomadism to the agricultural life, Vico turned to the imaginary hypothesis of the first thunderclap and the sudden cult of Jupiter Tonans. But does this mean that the many tribes that are still savage and even today live naked and in cannibalism have never heard the sound of thunder? Vico had noted correctly, and was the first to do so, that the world of the nations had to be explained by the laws of the intellect; but on the basis of this fine principle, he subjected the laws of the intellect to the chance of meteors, and left the initial problem unsolved for analysis.

3. It always appeared to me that the ineffectiveness of our studies is due to the method favoured by the founders of Psychology, who, in order to know the human faculties, began to scrutinize them most intimately in the conscience or self. But it seems to me that to be able to appreciate the maker, it is opportune to study the works, that to know the *faculties*, or the abilities to *make*, it is appropriate to study the *deeds* executed in practice; that for this reason it is preferable to inspect the entire circuit traced out by the sciences, as far as the most peripheral point discovered by them, and see the special action of which faculties can be discerned in them. The centre is determined once the circumference has been mapped out, not vice versa. In the psychological centre, everything is unified and merges together in a vague, unspecified capability, whereas out on the broader circle of the scientific circumference, all the *deeds* of the intellect can be marked out distinctly, and through them, its faculties can be plotted incontrovertibly, it being evident that *he who did was able to do*.

There are certain forces within us, to which no part in the origin of our ideas has ever been ascribed. Rather, we consider them to be extraneous to our intellect; and yet, if we look at the facts, we find them to have been most powerful causes in every scientific work of ours.

Consider *instinct*. Instinct is a faculty to perform certain actions without prior knowledge. Instinct is action without the idea. It is an ability which for this reason may indeed be said to be extraneous to the intellect. And yet many of our instincts cannot be said to be superfluous and indifferent to the overall elaboration of our knowledge.

The man who discovered the first geometrical theorem could have invented the second and third as well, he could have developed all scientific knowledge.[13] But the life of a man has a limit; his brief work is truncated by death. Therefore one geometrician had to succeed another and another, each building on the legacy of their predecessors, until eventually the entire chain of truths to be demonstrated was accomplished. Thus science had to become a tradition within a *stable society*.

Thales of Miletus[14] saw water as the element par excellence. We see water as a compound; we are sure of this, because we can unmake and reconstitute

---

[13] The theorem in question is attributed to Pythagoras (6th century BC).
[14] Thales of Miletus (c. 624/623 – c. 548/545 BC).

Lecture I – Idea of a Psychology of the Sciences

it: *The true is precisely what is made,* says Vico.[15] Could Thales have made such progress in his own time? Twenty-four centuries elapsed from Thales to Lavoisier, centuries which brought with them all the work of the science of the ancient Greeks and Arabs and the modern thinkers. The discovery of the composition of water was the last step in a long line of thoughts, in the building of which many generations collaborated.[16] It was not the work *of the solitary faculties* of one man, *rather that of the associated faculties of several individuals and several nations.*

A necessary truth of scientific construction is therefore that it must arise from within a society, or indeed *many societies,* so that if one should fall short on account of some adversity, the work may be continued by another.

For science to develop, then, all the faculties of the intellect would still not suffice, if man were not by instinct of nature a sociable being, that is, if he had not the instinct of the badger but that of the spider, which lives alone in the centre of its web. Seen in this light, instinct enters the work of science as a necessary cause.

And other instincts do the same, for instance, the need to communicate one's sentiments and thoughts, which we see in even the most uneducated of young women. This explains the spontaneous effort made to learn and form new words, a work which we carry on by assigning a new word to every new discovery: to oxygen, silicon, the locomotive. And if we analyse our languages, we find that the most abstract scientific terms are metaphors or derivatives from humble words of concrete and sensory origin. And if we push the analysis further and take the derivatives back to their roots, we find at the basis of all the most learned of languages a dead residue of a handful of monosyllables, most of which sound like imitations. Thus another human instinct comes into play, that of *imitation*; if we except certain species of birds and monkeys, it is one of the most characteristic instincts of the human species; and is of supreme importance not only in the formation of words, but of all disciplines in general. And this same instinct towards imitation, combined with others, explains the phenomenon of tradition, domestic and scientific, which gives rise to *the association between forefathers and heirs and that between teachers and students, and so to perpetual succession in the immortal work of knowledge.*

And there are other instincts too that can only be realized in society. These

---

[15] Translator's note: Giambattista Vico, *On the Most Ancient Wisdom of the Italians, Unearthed from the Origins of the Latin Language*. Including the Disputation with the *Giornale de' letterati d'Italia*, translated with an introduction and notes by L.M. Palmer (Ithaca-London: Cornell University Press, 1988), p. 46.

[16] Antoine-Laurent Lavoisier (1743-94).

are what the Scottish school calls *moral instincts* and what other schools of philosophy refer to as *sentiments*. They include credulity, adherence to friendship and authority, the love of praise, the terror of infamy.

Gentlemen, I am not reading you a treatise; I am putting forward a proposal for further study. The psychology of sciences, like that of languages, laws, religions and all institutions, is a branch of the *psychology of associated minds*, which I should like not to contrast with, so much as to superimpose on, the *psychology of the individual and solitary mind*. All thinkers felt it was impossible to rise to lofty abstractions and sublime truths from the individual intellect. So they were forced to supply more or less felicitous hypotheses, such as Plato's *anamnesis*,[17] which considered ideas as a faint memory of a previous life; such as innate ideas, such as Malebranche's vision,[18] such as the categories of thought prior to all thought, such as the idea of being as prior to every idea. But they were still unable to account for the difference between Polyphemus and Archimedes.[19] For Platonic reminiscences, innate ideas, the divine vision and the categories and idea of being were found in the unlearned cannibal Polyphemus as much as they were in the scientist Archimedes.

Gentlemen, the yeast which causes ideas to rise like bread does not do its work in one mind only; genius holds the hands of its precursors in a human chain. For ideas to rise, the most generous instincts must be expressed; minds must be stirred. The electric current of thought needs a battery made up of many hearts and intellects.

I must rush through these ideas. So I shall leave instinct for the moment, and touch briefly on sensation instead.

4. At first sight, sensation appears to be an area in which the savage life is strong and great. How often have we read of the wonders of the savage's acute eyesight being able to discern the enemy tribe's footprints in the sand? How to compare the weak, vacillating eyesight consumed in the nocturnal lamplight which Galileo extinguished in the lenses of his telescope?

Gentlemen, this is an illusion. Let us compare the whole range of sensations that present themselves to the mind of the savage and that of the scientist.

It is true that the life of the savage is absorbed by his senses; it is true that diligent exercise and harsh necessity make his senses vigil and acute. But even if he had the sight of an eagle and a dog's sense of smell, the sensations he ex-

---

[17] Plato (428/427-348/347 BC).
[18] Nicolas de Malebranche (1638-1715).
[19] Archimedes (287-212 BC).

periences would still be lacking in variety. They are the sensations that can be obtained within that horizon of woodland that encloses his customs, his fears. Few species of plants, the majority neglected and ignored by him because they are not useful for his few needs; few animals; the bank of a river, or lake; the caves and hovels which shelter his unclothed tribe; the traces of his enemies or their terrifying shouts. When we think of the primeval forests, our imagination is able to crowd the most various and manifold images into virtually a single point. But that is not what those forests are like. Every region has its own aspect; rainy or arid climates; the vast deserts of Australia, or the vast swamps of the Orinoco; oases scattered with palm trees; or Alps uniformly scattered with pine trees; prairies in which this or that family of grass is predominant, which look new and pleasing to those who arrive there for the first time, uniform and tedious to those who have always been there. In our country, more than five hundred vegetation species, around one-fifth of the flowering plants, belong to just two families of grasses and composites, most of which can barely be distinguished from one another even with the most diligent study.

But the kingdom of scientific sensations embraces all regions and every ocean; volcanoes and glaciers; plains and mountains; archipelagos scattered in the ocean, and the waterless desert. The animals of the various zones and individual continents, the camel and the reindeer, the elephant and the kangaroo parade before it, live in its stables or menageries; are catalogued in its museums, sketched and coloured on the walls of its houses. Which Samoyedic person ever saw the plants or animals or men of black Africa?[20] The savage can only see the things of his own nation; scientific sensation takes in the whole earth. Civilized man does not only receive sensations; he creates them. He drops anchor before the islands in the oceans, and deafens the savages with the thunder and lightning of his weapons. The light of his festive nights eclipses that of the stars. The colours of all metals, the lustre of all precious jewels; the flowers and fruits collected from all quarters and modified by artifice in infinite varieties of which nature is ignorant; the innumerable combinations of sounds and tempos, the whole creation of music, barely the first note of which is found in

---

[20] Cf. Cattaneo's "Sul principio istòrico delle lingue europèe", SL, I, pp. 154-201 (where the editor Piero Treves documents the essay's publishing history (p. 154, footnote 1)): "Herodotus called the peoples of the *forests (hylaea)* aboriginals; and beyond the steppes that surrounded them to the north, he described the peoples, of different descent and language, who were so uncivilized and wretched that they devoured each other, and he called them *Andròfagi*; the meaning of which, self-eater, is the same as the Slav name Samo-yed, which itself is the same as the Latin compound *Semet-edens*" (p. 168); in the same article Cattaneo locates the Samoyedic people in the region between the Arctic Ocean and the border with Asia (p. 164).

nature, are all new phenomena which the motor skills triggered by other, more sublime faculties provide to the sensitive one.

Even those sensations most closely related to the animal appetite change and multiply progressively with civilization. We do not think of it, but wine, bread, and all the thousands of combinations of tastes and smells are objects unknown to the savage life.

There is a world invisible to the naked eye, which is revealed to science by the telescope and the microscope. We are able to see the mountains on the moon, the phases of Venus, the pressures at the sun's surface, the bright points of the Milky Way and the nebulae. We discern the infinitesimal life forms that live in a grain of diamotaceous earth, that live in a drop of water, that swim in the aqueous humour of our pupils. The whole science of chemistry is a revelation of phenomena that are naturally inaccessible to our senses. What savage could see the green fumes of chlorine or the purple fumes of iodine rising from the dregs of a source of brackish water? This is a new order of sensations which science creates for itself.

And electrical equipment is like new senses; because with such equipment we are able to apprehend phenomena that elude those of our senses which we have by nature; we are able to engage in dialogue with powers whose presence in the universe the savage is unable to perceive. It is legitimate to suppose that as by nature we received a sense that perceives light vibrations and another that perceives sound waves, so too we could have been born with another organ which could have shown us how the compass makes magnetic oscillations. Perhaps it is some kind of internal sensory faculty of the type which directs certain species of rodents in their migration from the east to the west of Siberia. In any case, the person who gave us the magnetic needle to accompany us through the mists of the seas and the sandstorms of the desert, through the labyrinths of the mines, the person who extended electrical telegraph wires from one mountain slope to another, from one maritime coast to another, furnished us with the equivalent of another sense, as useful and real as the senses of sight and hearing. It is of no relevance if an organ is physically inserted in our brains, or if the new phenomena, represented spatially with the vibrations of a needle or a handset, *translate* to the sense of sight. For by it, our mind is initiated into an order of ideas which sight on its own was unable to give us, and which more than others is immersed in the secrets of the universe.

The few sensations which the savage has are sterile to intelligence, for they are vague, uncertain and immeasurable. The savage is unable to compare the heat of two summers, or the cold of two winters. We can, using instruments, measure how cold changes from frost to frost, and how heat changes from one fire to another. We know at exactly what temperature lead melts, iron melts, how many calories have to accumulate in a season in order to cause a bunch of grapes to ripen. Macedonio Melloni's device measures the infinitesimal amount of heat added by a person entering a room from the opposite side.[21] Thus we see sensory phenomena proliferate beneath the hand of science; but each of them remains the subject of individual perception. For there are phenomena that an individual on their own could never perceive in all their fullness, even with the help of instrumentation, without the sensory faculties of many other individuals associating with them as well. The men who saw the return of Halley's comet are not the same ones who saw it when it arrived the first time, seventy-five years ago.[22] In order to determine the area over which an earthquake is felt, several people must inform each other that they felt the tremors at the quake's furthest extremes. The observers who explore the magnetic tension of the earth's globe at various stations *are like parts of the civilized nations' common sensorium*.

Gentlemen, the splendid empire of sensation is not found in the savages' senses; it is found in experimental science, supported by all its most wonderful instruments, camped out on the mobile domes of its observatories. The power of science is displayed in the exercise of all faculties, and reaches its culmination in the development of the reflexive faculties. I shall submit this matter to your attention in another lecture.

---

[21] Macedonio Melloni (1798-1854). Cf. Cattaneo's "Della nuova nomenclatura proposta da Macedonio Melloni per dinotare le sue scoperte sul calorico radiante", *SST*, pp. 299-302 (first published anonymously in Il Politecnico V. XXVI (1842), pp. 178-81).

[22] Edmund Halley (1656-1742).

LECTURE II
On the Formation of Systems

Notes

The invitation sent by the Institute was for midday on Thursday, 23 August 1860, for a lecture entitled "Social Psychology: – On the successive formation of systems".[1]

Cattaneo clarified what was meant by the "successive formation of systems" in the lecture itself, when he states that his subject will be the "succession of systems" that "constitute ongoing, unlimited progress".

On the same day, the *Gazzetta di Milano* gave notice that Garibaldi and his soldiers had occupied Reggio and were now in charge of the Strait of Messina.

Before leaving Lugano for Milan, Cattaneo had written to Luigi Daelli to inform him of his arrival:

> For Thursday evening [23 August] we shall see what to do in due course. Tell our friends I'm not interested in lunches or other occasions where I'd have to engage in more or less pretentious and frivolous conversations. I have an inborn aversion to effusions of any kind. And things seem to me to be pretty serious, too serious for me to have to play the clown in whatever way.[2]

Cattaneo spent the night of 22 August in Monza, travelling into Milan the following morning (23 August). He described his meetings and impressions to his wife Ann as follows:

---

[1] *ACM*, cart. 19, pl. IX, copy of the invitation sent to Cattaneo in Lugano.
[2] *EP*, III, p. 379, letter dated 20 August 1860 and addressed to G.D. [Gino Daelli], (*ACM*, cart. 2, pl. XX). Luigi (Gino) Daelli (1816-82).

J'ai été a l'Institut, j'y ai trouvè bea[u]coup d'amis, entr'autres Benelli qui a 74 ans, et Ottavio Ferrario.³ Il y avait M.me Laura Mantegazza; sons fils docteur qu'a ètè en Amerique a lu une Mémoire.⁴ J'ai vu beaucoup de monde, et tous m'ont traité très bien; ils desirent toujours que je me fix ici. [...] La chaleur est trés forte. [...] Adieu ma chére, Garibaldi est a Reggio. Tu vois que desormais je peux l'attendre sans passer la mer.⁵

In September, less than a month after delivering the lecture to the Institute, Cattaneo was invited to work with Garibaldi, so he set off for Naples where he began work on projects that included the new railways in southern Italy. Cattaneo had been elected a member of parliament in March 1860, but had not attended the sessions themselves, confining himself to making criticisms and proposals from a distance. In the same year he threw himself with passion into editing and contributing a host of varied articles analysing issues of public utility and interest in depth to the newly relaunched *Il Politecnico*. It is sufficient in this regard to mention his writings on the railways, public education, the death penalty, the improvements to be made in Sardinia, and the administrative overhaul required.

On philosophical issues he published the following articles in the course of the same year: "Prolusione a un corso di filosofia civile" (VIII. 43, pp. 60-71); "L'uomo nell'universo. L'uomo nello spazio" (VIII. 46, pp. 343-65); "L'uomo nel tempo" (VIII. 47, pp. 453-68); and "L'uomo nell'ordine" (VIII. 48, pp. 596-606).

The previous year Cattaneo had published an anonymous essay entitled "Frammenti di filosofia civile, (1852-1859) – I sistemi" in *Il Crepuscolo* (31 May 1859, X. 10), The essay included a section on antithesis and antinomies, which in his lectures to the Institute he preferred to treat separately. Under the same headline and in the same journal Cattaneo had published "Del pensiero come principio di pubblica ricchezza" (15 April 1859), one of his densest and liveliest essays, in which he brings his learning to the subject of thought as a source of economic wealth, and intelligence and the will in associated minds. The essay

---

³ Ottavio Francesco Ferrario (1787-1867).

⁴ Laura Solera Mantegazza (1813-73); Paolo Mantegazza (1831-1910).

⁵ *EP*, III, p. 381, letter dated 23 August 1860 and addressed to Ann. (Translator's note: "I went to the Institute, I met a lot of friends there, including Benelli, who is 74, and Ottavio Ferrario. Mme Laura Mantegazza was there; her son, who is a doctor who has been in America, read out a paper. I saw lots of people, and everyone was very nice to me, they still want me to come back and live here. […] It's very hot […]. Goodbye my dear, Garibaldi has reached Reggio. See, now I can wait for him without even having to cross the sea.")

Lecture II – On the Formation of Systems

"refers explicitly to the philosophy course which Cattaneo had given in the cantonal high school in Lugano from 1852", notes Lacaita.[6] Both Bobbio (*SF*, II, p. 252-53, footnote *a*) and Castelnuovo Frigessi (*OPS*, IV, p. 138) point out the parallels between much of this lecture and the psychology lesson given in Lugano on the same subject (see *SF*, II, pp. 252-67).[7]

The lectures delivered in Milan obviously derive much of their material from the lessons given in Lugano, but in one sense the opposite is also true. Giancarlo Reggi, who until recently taught in the same Swiss high school in which Cattaneo gave his lessons, has suggested that the course which he taught is itself in some ways the product of the *Istituto Lombardo*: "In one sense the *Istituto Lombardo di Scienze Lettere e Arti* was the father of the cantonal high school in Lugano. Relations with the Milanese academy were never entirely interrupted."[8]

---

[6] Lacaita (2003).

[7] F. Geymonat (2018, p. 93) analyses Cattaneo's use of this term, noting that: "Cattaneo's choice was to avoid using the Italian equivalent of *système* in a political context, preferring to reserve the use of this borrowing from Greek for speculative vocabulary, for which he was authorized by Galileo's previous use of it".

[8] Reggi (2003, pp. 89-148).

Figure 4   On the Formation of Systems, manuscript's first page.

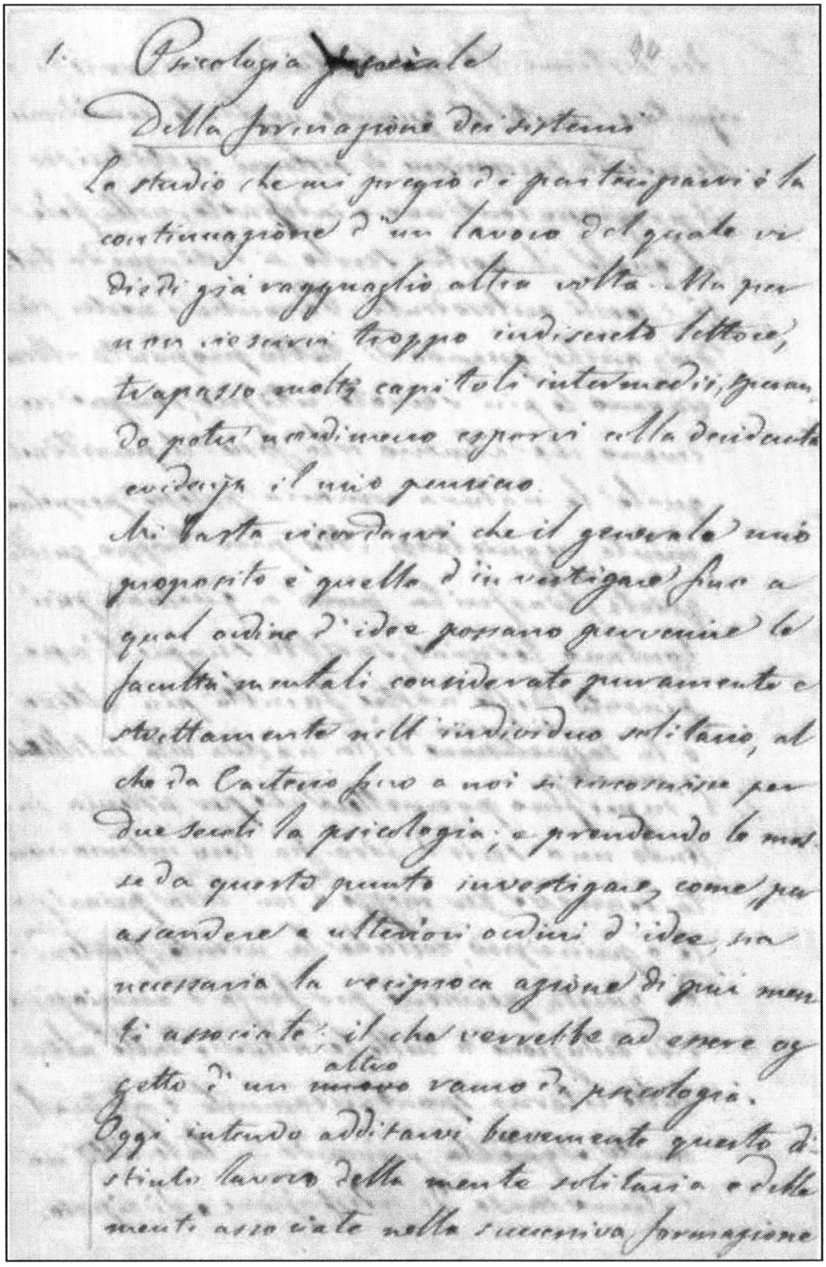

Copyright Comune di Milano – all rights reserved – Milano, Palazzo Moriggia | Museo del Risorgimento

On the Formation of Systems

The study which I am pleased to share with you here is the continuation of the work of which I informed you previously. But so as not to prove too importunate an orator, I shall omit many of the intervening chapters, while hoping to expound my thought to you with the desired clarity nonetheless.

Suffice it for me to remind you that my general intention is to investigate what order of ideas can be reached by the mental faculties considered purely and strictly in the solitary individual, to which psychology has been confined for two centuries, from Descartes to our own day;[9] and then, building on this, to show how, in order to ascend to further orders of ideas, the reciprocal action of several associated minds is necessary, which would hence become the subject of another branch of psychology.

Today my intention is to describe briefly to you how the solitary mind and associated minds work differently in the successive formation of systems. You will not find this subject of study useless, if it is considered that such a succession of systems is what constitutes ongoing, unlimited progress, and that it is by its faith in such progress that our century is distinguished from all previous ones. For even when our forefathers wholeheartedly embraced the most distant utopias, they still believed that such utopias would be the point at which human nature could eventually rest forever. However, such rest, even deferred to some more distant term, would always mean that our most active faculties were to go into slumber, and our intellectual and moral life was to be cut off.

1. There is no need to specify that I take system here to refer to a series of ideas connected intimately to each other by means of a principal idea or a principle, so that, by starting from it, the mind cannot help but arrive, by means of asso-

---

[9] René Descartes (1596-1650).

ciation and deduction, at all others; and then, from these others, return spontaneously and habitually to it, experiencing an intimate sense of satisfaction and rest in such an act.

2. The tendency to co-ordinate ideas around a principle is by nature consistent with our intellect.

Firstly, every object of our perceptions is already part of the same universe; and for this reason our perceptions are already related to each other in a system. The idea of putting several flowers together in a bunch is stimulated by the natural similarity that exists between one flower and another; with this, the solitary mind has reached only the idea of genus, but already it points, albeit from a huge distance, to the principle based on which, in the fullness of time, Linnaeus was to order the entire plant system. All objects that stimulate ideas in us, forming part of a natural order, tend to form themselves into a system within us, for the simple reason that they are already part of a system outside us. It depends not on our minds but the external world.

Secondly, as man, due to the limited nature of his mind, is unable to represent many distinct things simultaneously, he is forced to combine many ideas in a single concept; and so tends necessarily to reduce things to *genera*, and facts to *laws*, and genera and laws to increasingly comprehensive *orders* and *systems*, always aspiring to unity even when he does not have the ability to grasp it.

Thirdly, the individual mental faculties, sensation, memory, attention, reflection are not separate entities but a single thinking entity performing different actions. Of all these different actions, it has but a single consciousness, in which even the most disparate ideas testify to each other, and associate with each other in various ways as a result of both intrinsic similarity and outright opposition, and also extrinsic circumstances of place and time, so that the presence of one inevitably brings to mind the other.

Fourthly, as universal ideas such as space, time, number, being, substance and action are repeated in every genus, these serve to connect all genera under a common aspect. From these universals we pass, by means of deduction, to others that are still linked to the former; and all those objects in which we notice them are also connected to them.

Fifthly, many reflexive operations, such as synthesis, classification and deduction, involve bringing ideas together, ordering them and connecting them in various ways; which prepares, so to speak, the various threads to be woven into systems.

Therefore, because man lives in the presence of a *single universe*; because of the *limited* nature of his *intellect*; because of the *oneness* of his *consciousness*: be-

Lecture II – On the Formation of Systems

cause of the *identical nature* of the *universals*: and because of the *overall* effect of all *reflexive* operations, he would tend to make his notions into a system even if we imagined him to be entirely isolated, like Condillac and Bonnet's thinking statue.[10]

But let us consider man in his rightful place, the place which he occupies in the great chain of being, as a naturally and spontaneously gregarious genus like the antelope, as a social animal like the beaver, as a family animal like the dove. Even in spontaneous and primitive life, even if the intellect barely floats above the natural animal's instincts, it already tends towards systems. The savage barely knows the climate of his own skies, the woods and sands of his country; he is enclosed in an island in the midst of an endless ocean; and yet, driven by those internal powers that are inseparable from his being, he already makes what surrounds him into a system. Even he has something to add to what his senses tell him regarding the sun and the moon, the wind and the rain, the grass and the animals.

And where does the savage find the idea or principle around which to unify all others? The savage, diligently scourged by the necessities of life, concerns himself only with what is necessary for life. Everything that is neither food nor drink, everything that is not hunting or battle, everything that cannot harm his enemy or be of use to that group of living beings with which he identifies, is as though nothing to him; he neither sees it nor hears it. All travellers have noted this lack of interest in the savage for everything that does not fall within the narrow circle of his own thoughts. Whereas hunger, thirst and fatigue, or equally fear, love and vengeance, always call him back to himself and his own. There is a voice that appeals uniquely and assiduously to his conscience, the voice of selfishness, which science calls *ego*; this ego is surrounded first by the family, then the friendly tribe, and around both family and friendly tribe, the enemy tribe then winds itself like a crown of thorns. Passion predominates over the intellect; ideas germinate only insofar as passion is able to incubate them.

---

[10] Étienne Bonnot de Condillac (1715-80); Charles Bonnet (1720-93).
Cf. the Swiss psychology lessons, chapter III, "Della sensazione", *SF*, II, p. 151, where Cattaneo noted: "In this connection we should remember the ingenious method which Condillac (in his *Treatise on the Sensations*) and Bonnet (in his *Analytical Essay on the Faculties of the Soul*) devised by which to perform analysis on the operations of thought. They imagined they had a man before them, motionless like a *statue*; who had never before experienced any sensation; and at the time had only the sense of smell and that the first sensation was awakened in him by offering him a flower". Cattaneo himself, by contrast, argued that for cognitive purposes the senses operate together and not individually, and that the sensory and motor systems operate in relation to each other, not alone.

The first system, at the very point where it emerges from the ego, is already a social system.

With this principle, which is a principle of sentiment and not reason, a mere association of ideas and not the work of reflection, man explains to himself all the phenomena with which he is concerned and which he notices; all the others remain outside his system. I call it a *closed* system. A system which is undisturbed by external influence, could remain closed forever. And to tell the truth; after thousands of years since the human age began on this earth, there are tribes in Australia and equatorial America even today which have not found the numbers to count on the fingers of one hand. Many peoples have perished without ever escaping primitive barbarism.

The savage's philosophy interprets nature through the will; because the will is a principle close to instinct, of which even savage life itself is conscious. Everything that moves appears to be alive; the animal, even the plant appears to be transformations of man. In Aesop's morality, animals feel and think like men do. And where Aesop's fable is able to serve as morality, metempsychosis is able to become theology.

I say can become; but when? And how? What is the opportunity that can bring about this or some other new course of thought in the barbarian intellect? And around what principle can a new system be built?

The principle is again sentiment. Among the most wretched tribes, there is always, in the individuals or families, some slightly higher degree of strength, courage or wisdom, or even only ambition and ferocity. There is always someone who leads where the others follow, who rests while the others are awake, who judges when the others are competing, who receives a larger share of the hunt or prey. His less difficult life may become somewhat comfortable, comprise even that which does not involve only hunger and thirst. His ego, conscious of such barbarian honours and powers, already conceives the idea of an order which he feels to be a principle in his tribe; and attributes a similar order to those wills which he believes to be dominant in nature as well.

In this new man who stands out from society, sensory faculties which are less beset by needs leave greater room for the imagination. The imagination fills every space that sensation does not occupy beforehand. Fantasy always develops systems; even in the latest ages it provides the hypotheses which often serve as the principle. The round sun and moon brought to mind the faintest idea of a human face; fantasy painted it; two bodies were outlined faintly, one male, the other female; so we had the sun and the moon, brother and sister; virtually all cases of the barbarous tribe were translated into the language of the stars; eclipses came to be seen as a mortal struggle with some invisible monster;

when the moon no longer shone, she was believed to have descended to earth, compelled by some potent voice or secret love. Human societies, in the fertile valleys alongside the great rivers and lakes, came to associate with one another and multiplied, scattered to other regions, found other fruits, discovered grains, tamed the horse and bull, invented the chariot; and fantasy bit by bit continued its work; it gave horses and a chariot to the sun as well, to the moon, the dawn and the night.

So, with the victories of the senses and reason, the legacy of dreams grew too. Discovery could not contend with the tradition of error amid which it was imperceptibly and almost secretly developing. Fantasy still held the majority of the social system in everything which did not fall directly under the criterion of sense; it was truth that appeared to be a dream to the masses. Is it not true that even today we often speak of the truth as a utopia? Father Caccino was able to deride Galileo to his fellow citizens with the following words: *Viri Galilei quid statis adspicientes in cælum?*[11] And Democritus, the man of genius who was the first to see a myriad of distant stars in the Milky Way, seemed to be a man who spoke only in order to taunt those who listened to him.[12] To the multitudes, the truth appeared to be that the Milky Way was a trail of milk spilt by the goddess Hera; or that it was a furrow burnt into the fields of heaven by the errant chariot of Phaethon, son of Helios; and to the serious and wise Romans, Ovid was able to repeat the myth it was the great way that led the heavenly dwellers to the palace of Jupiter:

Hac iter est superis ad magni tecta Tonantis.

M 1.108.[13]

---

[11] Father Tommaso Caccini (1574-1648) pronounced an invective against Galileo in the church of Santa Maria Novella in Florence, on the fourth Sunday of Advent in 1614, including a play on words from St Luke's Acts of the Apostles, and arguing that "geometry is one of the arts of Hell, and that mathematics should be banned from all states on the grounds that it is a source of heresy" (C. Cantù, *Schiarimenti e note alla Storia Universale*, vol. VI (Turin: Pomba, 1844), p. 588). Cf. "Lettere della figlia di Galileo, scritte a suo padre", attributed to C. Arduini and Cattaneo, which describes Galileo's scientific, literary, human and family formation, in *SSG*, III, pp. 248-66, (originally published anonymously in Il Politecnico XVI. LXXIX (1863), 70-82; for the attribution to Arduini and Cattaneo, cf. *BC*, p. 78). (Translator's note: the biblical reference is to Acts 1.11, "Men of Galilee [...] why do you stand here looking into the sky?".)

[12] Democritus (c. 470/457 – c. 370 BC).

[13] Ovid, *Metamorphosis*, I. 170. (Translator's note: "This is the road which the gods must take to the mighty Thunderer's royal palace": Ovid, *Metamorphoses*, trans. by David Raeburn (London: Penguin, 2004), p. 13.)

And we too, even us, in repeating these elegant dreams, hear some indescribable pleasure in our mind.

The various primitive systems which peoples shaped, always agree with each other in certain respects. This is because nature, even in the most diverse areas, displays many identical laws and similar circumstances; and because mankind, even between peoples equipped most unequally by nature, has similar perceptive and reflexive faculties. This is what Vico called *the common nature of nations*; whereby the same ideas are found among peoples which could not have communicated them to each other.

Each one of these social systems contains some part of the truth, contains the knowledge of some natural fact which is useful to man. One people will have discovered wheat; another will have discovered iron. One will have observed the stars to guide them on the seas, another to feed their superstitions or to give themselves courage in their misadventures. If two peoples come to communicate with each other as an effect of conquests, slavery, trade, kinship or studies, the discoveries made by one of the two will be added to the truths discovered by the other. The new parts of the truth banish those false and imaginary ideas which occupied their place in those minds. The other fantasies remain. The parts of the two systems, true and imaginary, that are able to be reconciled are gradually collected together in a new system. This new system is passed down as tradition; and if some other new innovation does not soon overtake it, the system is completed and closed, and public reason comes to settle on it. The new system is progressive; that is, it corresponds to the order of nature and morality more faithfully, if the new element is *true*. But if the new element is a new dream, if it is the fantastic assertion of a Mohammed, if it is despotism taking the place of liberty, if it is authority putting itself in the place of reason, then the system is regressive. There is progress in nations, but there is also regression and decadence; it cannot be denied that many lands which once flourished are now desolate; and many peoples have perished. But while our forefathers did not believe in progress, it is almost as though we no longer believe in decadence. Progress prevails because over the course of time, the number of truths grows naturally too. In general, a system which is subsequent to another embraces a greater quantity of discoveries. Sometimes, even as a result of great calamities, a people can be driven almost forcibly under the light of new truths. Thus a more powerful principle is conceived, for man is able to do as much as he knows.

Rome, at its origins, found itself at the confine of three languages: Latin, Sabine and Etruscan, each of which represented its own system of ideas. If we compare each of these three peoples, Rome had the more comprehensive and vaster system; in bringing families of these three peoples within its confines,

Lecture II – On the Formation of Systems

Rome brought together three systems which would become a single one: it could avail itself of the ideas of three peoples; and to these were added those of other, more distant peoples as well, such as the Carthaginians and the Greeks. Intelligence and valour being equal, its counsels had to prevail; this consistent advantage ultimately could not help but lead it to subdue rival forces and absorb them.

Thus constituted from its origin, Rome continued to be open at all times to the ideas of other peoples; it embraced them, it did not reject them like China or India did, which had been constituted with exclusive systems from their origins. China imposed its traditions on its conquerors as well.

A few miles from Rome, the Greek cities were scattered on all the shores of Italy; this was the mission assigned to the decemvirs, to open the Roman laws up to the Greek experience.[14]

At the mouth of the Tiber, a Carthaginian ship ran aground; and Rome immediately made a model out of it.[15] Why do the Chinese today not do the same thing? Why do they take on steam-powered ships with their inept junks? Later on, Stoic philosophy was poured into Roman jurisprudence in floods.[16] A perpetually open system could continue for several centuries to accumulate in itself all those advantages which in other nations remained disjointed and incomplete. Ultimately, whatever was to be found in the weapons, politics, agriculture, trade and philosophy in the cities of the Etruscans, the Druidic orders,[17] the arsenals of the Carthaginians, and the schools of Greece, everything became the legacy of a people which was greater than the others, because it took into itself all things that made all the other peoples great.

But however great an abundance of ideas a nation manages to combine into its system, once it has completed the work and succeeded in reconciling and

---

[14] This is an allusion to the Roman laws in the Twelve Tables. Elsewhere Cattaneo seems to suggest he was in agreement with Vico's thesis: "Contrary to what all historians were saying, Vico had the courage to deny that the Romans could have obtained the twelve tables of their ancient laws from Athens; the similarity of these tables with ancient Greek law could only have been the result of similar civil circumstances". Cf. Cattaneo, "Su la 'Scienza Nuova' di Vico", *SF*, I, p. 112 (originally published in Il Politecnico II. IX (1839), pp. 251-86, then with a different title in other editions; cf. *SF*, I, p. 95, footnote *, and Fugazza, 2018, p. 50, footnote 5). Vico had arrived at his theory as a result of the implausibilities and anachronisms in the tradition of the decemvirs' Twelve Tables.

[15] The Romans adopted the *quinquireme*, with five banks of oars, after adopting the Carthaginian model during the First Punic War.

[16] Cf. *SF*, III, "Del diritto e della morale", footnote 1, pp. 357-67, where Cattaneo describes the Greek schools of philosophy that influenced Roman law.

[17] Orders of priests among Celtic peoples.

co-ordinating all its ideas, it tends to stop and settle in that state of mental repose. And it may remain there, inactive, for many generations, until some new principle counters it, disconnecting the old system and reforming it around a new fabric.

Meanwhile, the place of those members of the active and industrious generation who die is gradually taken by other generations, who, through inheritance and passive imitation, collect ideas that have already been developed. The heirs' mental and moral faculties have no opportunity to ferment or labour; they are like plants in the winter season; they have no leaves, flowers or fruit; no poetry, wisdom, valour or virtue. This is what happened with the great Byzantine unity; this is what happened in China with the Confucian school of thought, twenty-four centuries after Confucius.[18] All issues appear to have been already resolved by the wisdom of the *elders*; wretched are the children who are afraid to do better than their fathers; the most audacious theories in time are reduced to arid rules, old formulae, stupid, servile habits. However, *the same order of ideas* that at one time was *progressive* thereafter becomes *decadent*. Peoples need new work all the time to keep their faculties alive and awake. Systems must always keep themselves *open*; a finished, closed system becomes the graveyard of the intelligence and virtue which wove it together in the first place. The Asians fell into such a torpor, as a result of that same, precocious wisdom which is admired in their ancient systems. Greece lay in the same state for a thousand years, after the ceaseless agitation of the rival republics was replaced by funereal pyramid of the holy Byzantine empire, following the Macedonian conquest and imperial unity. The supreme worth of experimental science lies not merely in the prodigious feats of physics and chemistry, in the sense that they are true benefits to the material part of our existence, but in shaking up and renewing the systems, they keep our faculties in diligent tension, and set before the barbarous or stationary nations the harsh alternative of either associating themselves with progress, or succumbing; and so, in this their apparent ruin, also associating themselves with us and our future.

Where a people which has just emerged from barbarism and has barely any apparatus in terms of ideas; but turns with generous faith to new ideas, and uses and exalts all its faculties regarding them, it may soon come to prevail over an older and more indoctrinated people, whose faculties are constrained by the authority of the past. An *open* system can resemble perpetual youth, which is exactly what every experimental science is. For this reason, ancient peoples become young again in the colonies, by virtue, precisely, of the systems, in parts

---

[18] On Confucius cf. Cattaneo, "Ideologia delle genti", *SF*, III, pp. 83-90.

Lecture II – On the Formation of Systems

new, which they are forced to implement. In Greek history, the Dorians, who in their mountainous homelands were virtually barbarian, displayed high political genius in the colony of Sparta; and only attained a full life of the mind in the overseas colonies of Halicarnassus, Rhodes, Taranto and Syracuse.

In certain combinations of ideas, brought by the political and commercial mingling of the nations, principles in conflict with each other often come to turn in on themselves. In such cases the effort to reconcile them in stable and peaceful systems becomes perpetually vain.

In the capital of ideas which modern Europe inherited from all peoples of antiquity and the Middle Ages and to which it gradually added its own discoveries, there are many principles which are more or less in conflict with each other. Such, for example, are Roman and feudal jurisprudence; the philosophies of the Greeks and the theocracy of the Hebrews; mathematics and poetry; physics and metaphysics; the needs of the state and the infallibility of the church; disdain for worldly things, and the cult of riches. Furthermore, the experimental process, fertile with discoveries, and political rivalry, greedy to profit from them, continually encourages even the sleepiest nations and the most backward of governments to embrace an always renascent and inexhaustible series of innovations; which penetrate and prise open even the most compact of systems.

Following the renaissance of sciences, minds which were forced to combine so many discordant thoughts made themselves acute, audacious and free through such continuous effort. They acquired the power to emancipate themselves from every closed system and to shake off every yoke of authority, resolutely and fearlessly following only the light of experience and reason. Experience and reason give rise to endless new discoveries; to continuous mobility and uncertainty of systems, unless they are able to justify themselves by their usefulness; whence the continual need for new elaborations and discoveries.

And so in Europe an expansive force presses and harries the traditional systems, both those of the barbarous nations whose faculties have never been exercised, and those of the *ancient* nations whose faculties have fallen back into slumber. The irreconcilable opposition of the principles embraced confusedly in Europe, the inexhaustibility of the experimental process, and the reason of the peoples, now released from every bond of tradition, prepare humanity for an indefinite career, and promise it perpetual youth.

Progress, to the same degree that it provides new ideas, provides also new employment for the intellect, keeps our moral faculties in enforced exercise, and drives them on to continuous perfection.

With this auspicious prospect, I shall draw to a close the deduction of my thoughts, which are already too verbose.

LECTURE III
On Antithesis as a Method of Social Psychology

Notes

Cattaneo delivered no lectures to the Institute in 1861 and 1862. Despite the offers received, he did not return to Milan to teach, but devoted himself to writing essays and articles instead. Having received a mandate to act as consultant to the government, he took part in the commission to revise the tax laws of Canton Ticino; and advocated in word and deed on behalf of the Gotthard route as the best transalpine railway link.

He resumed the sequence of lectures on Thursday, 12 November 1863, presenting his colleagues at the Institute with "another portion of the work, now nearly finished, on the *Psychology of Associated Minds*, namely: 'On Antithesis Considered as a Method of Psychology'".[1] He repeatedly expressed his intention to bring his work on associated minds together to form a single collection, and continued to do so in the next three lectures as well, all of which formed part of the overall design.

The following month (20 December) Cattaneo sent the text to Giulio Curioni:[2] "A thousand apologies for the unintended delay, enclosed are the *corrected proofs* of my last lecture which I entrust to your tender care".[3] The text, defined "Memoria" (Essay), was printed in ATTI IL, III (1862-63), 450-54, with the title "On Antithesis as a Method of Social Psychology", following a brief introductory note. In this case it was the full essay with the complete text, rather than merely an abstract.

---

[1] *EP*, IV, p. 173, letter dated 16 October 1863 to the secretary's office of the *IL*.
[2] Giulio Curioni (1796-1878).
[3] *EP*, IV, p. 185, letter dated 20 December 1863, addressed to Curioni.

Cattaneo sent the version of the lecture to Adriano Lemmi,[4] who had it published on the first page of *Il Diritto. Giornale della democrazia italiana* (Turin, 24 December 1863), untitled and dated 23 December.

Swiss publisher Veladini published the pamphlet *"Dell'antitesi come metodo di psicologia sociale. Lettura del D.r Carlo Cattaneo all'Istituto di Scienze e Lettere di Milano nell'adunanza del 12 novembre 1863"* in Lugano with the date "1864"; this edition has a series of minor variants compared to the versions published previously.

Yet another version was published in *Il Politecnico* (February 1864, XX. 92-93, 262-70), with the title *"Dell'antitesi come metodo di psicologia sociale; lettura del dott. Carlo Cattaneo al R. Istituto Lombardo"*; this is the text that was reproduced in OEI (VI, pp. 311-24), as the note there states.

For the present edition, the version published by Veladini in Lugano has been used, for it seems likely that Cattaneo curated and edited the text himself as suggested by a letter which he sent to Agostino Bertani on 24 February 1864.[5]

Cattaneo's *lecture* on antithesis provoked a considerable reaction and harsh opposition in conservative Catholic circles. An anonymous author "professing the strictest Catholic faith" published a polemical pamphlet under the title *Pensieri filosofici sopra un discorso del signor dott. Carlo Cattaneo letto nell'Istituto di scienze e lettere in Milano nell'Adunanza del 12 novembre 1863*.[6] The publication was noted by Alessandro Levi in *Il positivismo politico*,[7] while the issue of clerical opposition to Cattaneo in Ticino was dealt with at length and in suitably documented fashion by Bobbio.[8]

---

[4] Adriano Lemmi (1822-1901).

[5] Agostino Bertani (1812-86). EP, IV, pp. 203-05, letter dated 24 February 1864, addressed to Bertani.

[6] (Translator's note: *Philosophical Thoughts on a Speech given by Dr Carlo Cattaneo to the Institute of Science and Letters in Milan at the Session held on 12 November 1863.*) Milan: Besozzi, 1865. The work is held in the library of the Civiche Raccolte Storiche of Milan City Council, catalogued as L300 ("Raccolta Bertarelli"). The lecture was written in 1863, the polemical pamphlet in 1864, and publication may be dated to 1865.

[7] Levi (1928), pp. 30-31, note A.

[8] Bobbio (1971, pp. 139-81) develops the issue of conservative clerical opposition in Canton Ticino. The issue is also discussed by Armani (1997, pp. 151-56) and Panzera (2004, pp. 549-61).

Figure 5 On Antithesis as a Method of Social Psychology, cover page, Lugano, 1864.

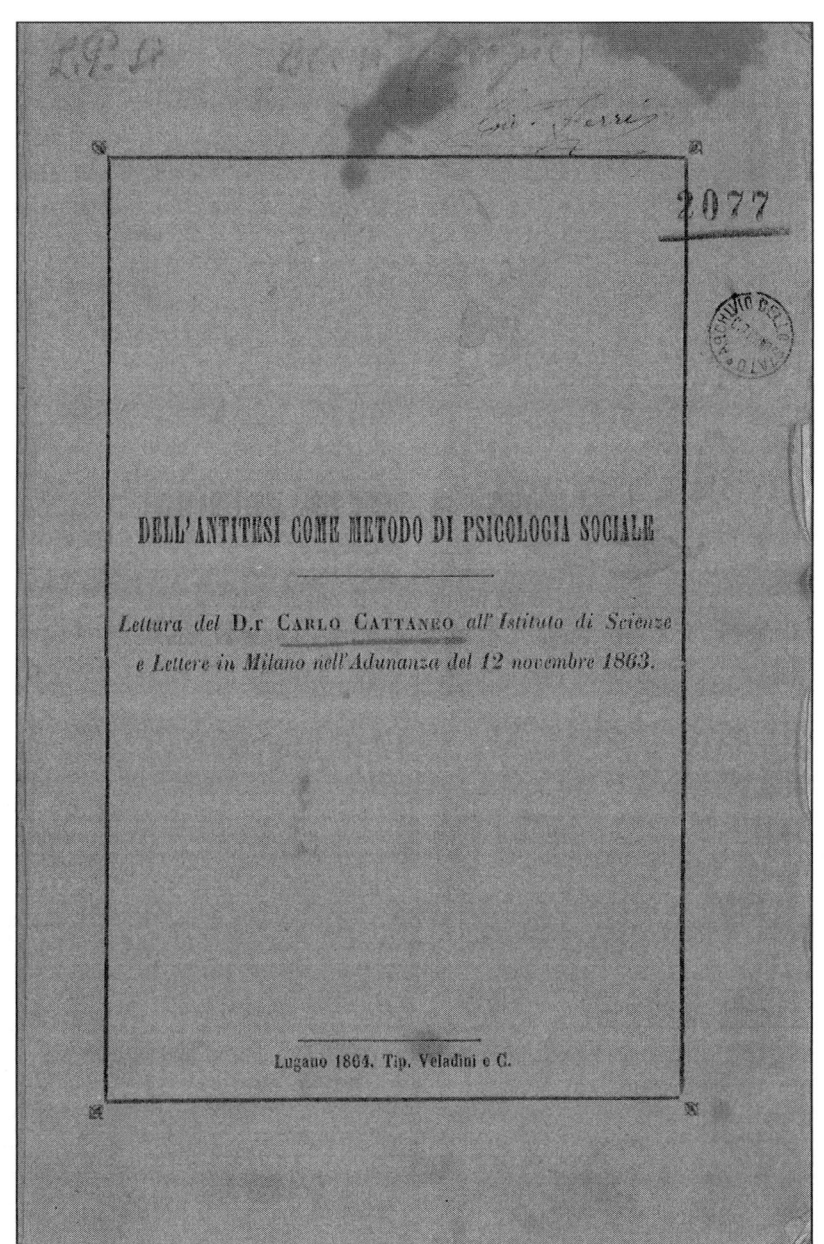

On Antithesis as a Method of Social Psychology

I shall continue to read from a work, some fragments of which I have already submitted to the attention of my generous colleagues. For this same reason, however, it is necessary for me to recall my fundamental thought to their memory.

Experimental philosophy has three fields: *nature*, the *individual*, and *society*.

The philosophy of *nature*, for the ancients, was no more than an imaginative prelude. Application of the new experimental method has led to such felicitous and continual discoveries, that a family of entirely new sciences established itself almost immediately, and continues to open up an increasingly vast and sure field of philosophical generalities.

Another glory of the times is the philosophy of *society*, since languages, legislations, religions, sciences, poetry and the arts have all become new fields of moral and intellectual observation.

The philosophy of the *individual*, though, is a different matter. In it, too, the experimental principle, which with reciprocal sensory substitution has already provided the basis of the education for deaf, dumb and blind people, is now pursuing new methods of analysis, in prisons and mental institutions as well, and in comparative analysis of the different human people groups. To some, however, it seems that in this way humanity is being examined in its exceptions, rather than in its normal and general being. To such people it appears that deep thinkers should not concern themselves with such varieties; that they should be relegated to the category of fortuitous and irrational phenomena; that the typical individual should be contemplated in its own conscience; or, that all free, solitary sources of humanity and science should be attributed to the individual, any individual (even a savage).

Descartes, indeed, distancing himself from tradition and society in favour of the pure, unadorned spirit, said: – "Do you not realize you are speaking to a spirit so released from bodily concerns that he does not even know whether or not there was another man before him?" – Descartes set little store by the senses, nor did he ascribe much value to the intellect's activity; he attributed only the lowliest of notions to them; all the most sublime ideas in his eyes were free and secret gifts of the nascent soul. It was God who gave ideas; God could change them, just as he could change the universe. If life was continual creation, thought was continual inspiration. Descartes' solitude paved the way for an entire theology.[9]

Thirty years after his death, Locke reclaimed the rights of philosophy over philosophy. He rejected the doctrine of innate ideas, seeking to show that reflection was sufficient for the individual to ascend from the sensory perception to any loftier order of ideas. He went further: – he showed how reflection, in its noblest efforts, was assisted by language.

Now language, I am sure you will concede gentlemen, is *society*.[10]

Hence Locke in fact drew his theory from three sources: *sense*, *reflection* and *language*; that is, from *nature*, the *individual*, and *society*.

But society contributes to the individual's thought in many other ways, not just language.

This had not been Locke's objective; he did not enter this field; nor did those said to be his successors enter it; nor did those said to be his opponents. Condillac and Tracy confined themselves to sensation and language. Out of love for simplicity, they endeavoured to do without reflection; however, they introduced an equivalent; the internal faculty which for Condillac *transforms* sensations; or judgement, which for Tracy *perceives* relations.[11] Kant and Fichte, by contrast, limited themselves to reflection, isolating it from even its most intimate sense, and so contemplating it as part of the concept of pure reason; but then both the former, with his *a priori* forms and categories, and the latter, with his continuing revelations, ended up returning to Descartes.

Social thought was only fully contrasted with individual thought by Vico, who was contemporary with Locke's old age. Vico studied man in the nations; each nation seemed to him to repeat, in their various places and times, the

---

[9] Cf. the Swiss philosophy lesson "Dell'idealismo", in *SF*, II, pp. 289-91.

[10] Cf. Cattaneo's lectures on linguistics (*SF*, II): "Della capacità dell'uomo a formarsi una lingua" (pp. 348ff.); "Dell'influenza del linguaggio nelle idee" (pp. 355ff.). On Cattaneo's contribution to linguistics and ethnolinguistics, see *Gli studi filologici, linguistici e orientali*, in *ILASL-III*, p. 14. On the relationship between individual languages and the human faculty of language, and on K.W. Humboldt's influence on Cattaneo's philosophy, cf. De Mauro (2004, p. 149). On Cattaneo as linguist, see F. Geymonat, (2018).

[11] Antoine-Louis-Claude Destutt de Tracy (1754-1836).

same course of ideas. A century later Hegel again took up the man-people ideology; breaking up Vico's circle, he replaced it with the more modern notion of progress; he also went further with the analysis, distinguishing the individual nations, trying to assign each of them the special realization of one of those ideas, the sequence of which is what constitutes ongoing progress.

Through the work of these two thinkers, it became clear how humanity was itself the source of those highest orders of ideas which peoples and schools had vainly attributed to the muses, sibyls, domestic gods, Socratic ecstasy, intuition, *anamnesis*, *gnosis*, innate ideas, or pre-established harmonies. Gentlemen, all the highest proofs of science and virtue are realized in the agreements and disagreements of men in close relation to each other. Humanity is like a battery, in which the electrical current does not originate from either the positive or negative pole, but from certain forms of contact between them. Humanity is the native environment of everything that appears superhuman in the thought of the nations. This concept is symbolized, in all its simplicity, in the biblical phrase: – "Where two or three are gathered in my name, there I am".[12] –

Vico and Hegel attempted the history of ideas in peoples, they attempted the *Ideology of society*. But they did not go further and describe the new *modes of action* in which society situated the individual's faculties; they did not get as far as the *Psychology of society*. It remained to be analysed by what other means, apart from language, minds associated with each other in families, classes, peoples, mankind, could work together with common intelligence, or against it; and how they came to operate with methods and results which for solitary minds would be impossible.

This *Psychology of associated minds* is the necessary link between the *Ideology of the individual* and the *Ideology of society*. It is to this new strand of research, to this neglected science *which can provide fresh support to the culture of the nations,* that I invite scholars. And now I shall put forward another part of my own contribution in this area.

So now, coming from the general argument to one of its chapters, I shall trace out in brief the reciprocal action which several minds have created when set in *antithesis* to each other, moved, that is, by contrary ideas.

Fichte saw antithesis when the individual quietens themselves in the depths of their conscience, and in so doing comes to discern the self from the non-self.[13] But from his perspective, he was unable to note that this non-self consist-

---

[12] Matthew 18.20.
[13] Cf. Cattaneo, "La guerra d'Italia. – Le costituzioni. Li operai nel mondo moderno. La filosofia di Fichte nel pensiero nazionale, di Ferdinando Lassalle. Berlin, 1859-62", in *SP*, IV,

Lecture III – On Antithesis as a Method of Social Psychology

ed of brute nature and human society combined. He failed to observe that in this non-self, the thoughts of others could be contrasted with our own. What he called antithesis was in fact only *distinction*: it was an act of analysis in the conscience; it was only *presence*, not *opposition*. And since the first intuition was one, its antithesis, discovered in it by means of analysis, could come to be joined again to the thesis; and in this way a synthesis could be arrived at, that is, a second intuition, in which the consciousness of the whole comes to embrace that of the parts.

The antithesis of associated minds is, to my mind, that act with which one or more individuals, in seeking to deny an idea, come to perceive a new idea; – or that act with which one or more individuals, in perceiving a new idea, come, even unconsciously, to deny another.

In the first case, what distinguishes the new idea is that it arises from the conflict of several minds, and that among minds in agreement, or in a mind on its own, it would not have arisen. For example, in a criminal sentencing, the conflict between prosecution and defence may lead to an unknown person being revealed as the guilty party. No-one can predict what the final consequence to which the negation of a philosophical, theological or political idea may reach will be. Without Locke's and Vico's negations, Descartes' idea would never have had the privilege of being the vital moment from which two new philosophies would originate, both of which lay outside the terms he had himself set. No-one would have foreseen that Luther's negation would lead to the thirty years' war, nor to the establishment of that permanent duality in Germany[14] which opened up three centuries of enlightened scientific ferment, after so many centuries of mental sterility.

In the second case, the new idea does not emerge in the form of opposition; it may exist for a long time without revealing its negative force. In chemistry, the discovery of oxygen was inevitably bound to remove the name of element from air, water and earth. But this was at no stage the intention of Cavendish or Priestley or Lavoisier.[15] Even after this discovery Priestley, who played such an important part in it, was tormented by the fact that oxygen harshly negated the fictitious phlogiston in which he had believed for so long. Equally, when Lavoisier introduced scales to the instrumentation used in chemistry, combining quantitative and qualitative analysis, he predestined himself and all others

---

pp. 374-99 (originally published in *Il Politecnico* XV (1862), pp. 190-209, and subsequently in other editions as well).

[14] Between Protestantism and Catholicism.

[15] Henry Cavendish (1731-1810); Joseph Priestley (1733-1804); Antoine-Laurent Lavoisier (1743-94).

to make it increasingly evident that nature proceeds by means of absolute numerical proportions.[16] Having demonstrated that chemistry is perennial order in the perennial vortex of transformations, the idea of matter as chaos could not help, at the proper time, but appear to be contradictory and irrational. So from that moment the Pythagorean numbers won the final victory over the metaphysics of the Eleatics, Platonists, Manicheans, Brahmans and Buddhists, for whom in everything underlying the senses, there is nothing that is enduring, fixed, certain or true, but everything is illusion and delirium. – Thus today, we see the dynamic theory of heat, virtually unknown in schools, unknown certainly in those in which we grew up, revealing the reciprocal commutability of heat and motion, thereby excluding the hypothesis of latent heat, that of fluid heat and any other notion of heat as substance; dissolving all the physics of imponderable fluids; combining the ideas of motion, cohesion, affinity, elasticity, magnetism, electricity, light, heat, stimuli and life into a single, supreme whole; replacing the principle of emanation with that of vibration; replacing the metaphysics of matter, ancient torment of the schools and terror of the theologians, with the metaphysics of forces: *Elohim*![17]

Sometimes the antithesis is only apparent; rival ideas survive; they share a realm which both aspired to conquer, shedding common light on other truths. – In medicine, the opposition of stimulus and contro-stimulus[18] led to the force of an illness being measured from its tolerance to remedies, to the opposite diathesis[19] being ascertained, and to specific varieties of both being discerned as a result. In geology, Neptunism and Plutonism are now so reconciled,[20] that no-one can deny any longer that the two powers are simultaneously at work in metamorphic rocks, glacial erratics, and in the inclinations and directions of strata, in the great mountains divided up by the Baltic and Mediterranean, despite being correlative in terms of direction and construction.

Sometimes the antithesis cancels out the opposite idea entirely. In physics,

---

[16] Cf. Cattaneo, "Varietà chimiche pei non chimici", *SST*, pp. 249-97 (originally published anonymously in *Il Politecnico* V. XXVI (1842), pp. 97-147).

[17] Hebrew name for God in the Old Testament.

[18] Cf. "Giovanni Rasori", in *SST*, pp. 87-8 (first published in *Annali di Statistica* (1837), signed "KK" and attributed to Cattaneo by Ambrosoli, 1960. p. 161), where the following comments were made on Rasori: "He established the doctrine of contro-stimulus, and from previously unobserved phenomena derived the wonderful and thoroughly true laws of pathological capacity".

[19] In medicine diathesis is a set of constitutional and functional characteristics that represents a predisposition to developing particular diseases.

[20] Geological theories on the origins of rocks.

the discovery of atmospheric pressure cancels out the poetic idea of abhorrence of a vacuum. In this case there is no reconciliation; Fichte's synthesis is not possible. On the contrary, in most cases the victorious antithesis goes beyond the confines of the original thesis; it spreads like fire, from error to error, destroying entire systems.

Then sometimes an entirely unforeseen antithesis attacks the victorious one. In astronomy, the idea of the earth's motion removed the sun from the ranks of the planets. But the recent idea that the sun itself, along with all its family, tends towards some point in the firmament, alters the assertion of the sun's absolute immobility; it contradicts the idea of the earth's return being via an identical orbit; it awakens the idea of a spiral orbit, similar, I should say, to the idea of progress itself, moving through spaces that are always new; alluding to the sublime idea that all the universe's physical and moral forces are eternally evolving.

The sun's motionlessness relative to the earth was thus the beginnings of the truth; but it brought with it a new form of error. This transitory form of an idea is referred to by some as relative truth; Fichte called those ideas which in other times must necessarily have appeared true, historical truths. But since this term awakens the insidious notion of a truth that is changeable, a truth that might not in fact be true, it is appropriate to retain the narrower definition of partial and incomplete truth. It was due to this kind of prudence that chemistry refrained from referring to un-decomposed bodies as elements; for a further step of analysis is always possible, that is, the hypothesis that the diversity of bodies is no more than a variety of tissues or density.

Sometimes, the lasting gain which antithesis procures for science is not truth itself but a method, an art, a habit which leads to the truth being discovered. Descartes was mistaken when he said that evidence is a criterion of truth. This, unfortunately, is not the case; evidence deceives mankind when it says that the earth is motionless. It is merely preliminary evidence. The criterion resides in the entirety of the evidence. Descartes changed the whole disposition of science through recourse to the method of geometrical simplicity, which replaced insidious dialectics.[21] He opened it up to all; as in the times of free Greece, he restored to all the right to understand and judge. So too Condillac exaggerated when he said that science is a well-constructed language. Unfortunately it is

---

[21] Bucchi (2018, p. 153) states that: "While Cattaneo was never sympathetic towards Cartesian psychology, which focused on the individual rather than social dimension of thought, he nonetheless never failed to acknowledge its importance in the scientific revolution which started in the seventeenth century".

not; chemistry, before becoming a language, had to perform a Herculean labour, between shadows and dreams, in search of gold and long life. But many years after Condillac's death, as a result of the keen influence of his philosophy, present at that stage to the French intellect only, the revolution imposed that nomenclature on the nascent discipline of chemistry in which the future discoveries of science were already resplendent in the names of things. For whoever was the first to call the binary compounds of sulphur sulphides, had already predestined that the binary compounds of chlorine and iodine, once they had been discovered and named, would be called iodides and chlorides; given the names, the idea itself is in part given. If only we had known, and if only we knew, how to turn these two sublime exaggerations by Descartes and Condillac to the advantage of other sciences.

For antithesis to become suitably productive, the considered work of several minds is necessary. An individual on his own can do no more than oscillate weakly in doubt between two as yet uncertain ideas; precisely for this reason, vital conflict can never be so resolute and powerful as when two individuals, factions or peoples clash, moved by opposite persuasions, boasting, offences or hatreds that one man alone could never conceive against himself. For antitheses often creep into our intellects almost surreptitiously, inspired by interests and passions. Unfortunately, however, in every council of legislators, there is always a general, stubborn antithesis which precedes all reasoning, indeed, all questions which are dictated by interests rather than by consciences. In the conflicts of life, reasoning is the reciprocal arm of all passions; pure reason is an act of analysis, an abstraction.

An amusing example is found in a text by a well-known contemporary of Machiavelli, in which two adversaries sitting in council in Florence are described. "[…]; and one of them, belonging to the Altoviti family, fell asleep. Then, although his adversary, who belonged to the Alamanni family, was not speaking and had said nothing, the person sitting next to him nudged him with his elbow, woke him up and said, for a laugh: 'Don't you hear what he is saying? Give your answer, because the Signori are asking for your opinion'. – Then Altoviti, very sleepy and not thinking what he was saying, got to his feet and remarked: 'My lords, I say completely the opposite to what Alamanni has just said'. – Alamanni replied: 'But I haven't said anything'. – And at once Altoviti retorted: 'Then to what you are going to say'. –[22]

---

[22] The episode is recounted by Baldassarre Castiglione (1478-1529) in his *Il Cortegiano*. (Translator's note: the transation here is taken from Baldesar Castiglione, *The Book of the Courtier*, trans. by George Bull (London: Penguin, 1967; reprinted 1976), pp. 181-82.)

Here we see a man who is determined, simply because of the presence of an adversary, to challenge an idea before he even knows what it is. One party has already decided to negate everything that the opposing party is about to put forward. But it cannot give rational form to its negative response without bringing forth all its dormant forces and developing a thought that would otherwise have been unattainable; and this, in turn, becomes the main motive force for the adversary's subsequent effort. Every objection commands a response; every act of reasoning commands another, logically correlative act of reasoning, which brings opposing ideas together in an inseparable embrace. Thinkers, when passions are engaged, become fighters; in the presence of an idea, they become blacksmiths, hammering away at the same iron; they are blind instruments of a common endeavour. Every new effort adds a link in the chain which pulls both parties further into the vortex of truth.

To a thinker, who first of all sweated to collect the science of his fathers, then to free himself from it, a lifetime is barely sufficient to be able to eventually bring forth a spark of his own thought from his mind; and with faithful love, and with fortune forsaking him, to feed it; to commend his name to that light and then die. The public life of Descartes lasted but thirteen years; Locke and Kant were already almost in their sixties when they brought their immortal thought to life. And if each of them had lived for a few years more, could they have waged war against themselves? Condemned the idea they had contemplated for so many years as just a dream? Broken the headstone of their own graves? No; to do this work of an enemy, another intellect, another will, another life was necessary. This is why the great thinkers, the ones who broke the circle of tradition and allowed their ideas to travel far and wide, almost always appear to be girded up as though for some exploit of war.

Only after the course of several generations, in scientific terms, does posterity realize how each of those thinkers had studied the same problem from a different aspect; how the chain of antitheses was in fact a series of partial analyses; how the different schools of thought, without wishing to and without knowing it, had divided up parts of the common analysis, all of them aspiring to conquer, in a first embrace, the entire circuit of universal synthesis.

Antithesis is not merely a method of scientific progress; it becomes a social principle in laws, governments and religions. Everyone today knows that the civil law which governs our households is a modern form of Roman law; which was the lengthy work of hereditary opposition. The praetor who aspired to become a consul, secured the vote of the majority by becoming a reformer, and by making his patrician privilege subordinate, in the praetorian edict, to his common right as a citizen.

The antitheses of politics echo down to philosophy. Rousseau, generous, poor and without honour, praised the savage life only in order to shame an unequal and inhuman society. De Maistre[23] and as many others as imagined themselves able to conquer philosophy, in truth were fighting the civil code that had abandoned the fief of the fideicommissum and the church to commerce.[24]

Antithesis penetrates nations with the art of war, for it forces them to make defence proportionate to attack, and vice versa; and harries them into making a series of mental and moral efforts. The person who first fashioned the sword, forced their enemy to equip themselves with another and to learn the art of skirmishing; the army which fashioned the first cannon commanded the architects to transform lofty walls into oblique, sunken bastions, and commanded the geometricians and physicians to make all the calculations of ballistics. Every discovery in artillery disrupts naval architecture; and likewise, all progress in ship-building forces artillery to perform new miracles.

Nor even is this the most important thing in the order of ideas. War constrains antiquated Asia to seek out new forms of militia. This brings with it a legion of new sciences, which link themselves inextricably to other orders of ideas, which in peoples' future destinies will be more powerful still. Whereas a barbarous instinct of conceit and avarice drives various nations to abuse the arms of civilization against the non-warfaring nations, from the antithesis of those rival desires, a new *jus gentium* is born. In the shadow of which, the Asian multitudes, educated in the veneration of static traditions, will find themselves involuntarily associated with us in the free life of trade and thought.

First handmaiden, then teacher, then enemy, philosophy wove itself inextricably into all theological deductions. The history of Christianity is a continual dispute between the innumerable factions, which proliferated from the ancient philosophies of the Orient and Greece. *Patriarchae haeresiarum philosophi;*[25] we find this phrase already written, as soon as the second century was coming to

---

[23] Joseph de Maistre (1753-1821).

[24] The reference is to the institutions of *fideicommissum* and mortmain, both of which constituted restrictions on free trade. On these, which Cattaneo described as "fiefs of the sword" and "fiefs of the cross", cf. "Ai liberi elettori, Lettera VII", 26 June 1867, *SP*, IV, p. 484-91 (originally published in *Gazzetta di Milano*, 28 June 1867); "Del diritto e della morale", *SF*, III, p. 372 and "Del pensiero come principio d'economia publica", *SE*, III, p. 360 (for the publishing history, see footnote * on p. 337); the latter was also published in Cattaneo, 2003.

[25] Tertullian, *Adversus Hermogenem*, 8.3: "haereticorum patriarchae, philosophi". (Translator's note: "[…] philosophers, those patriarchs of heretics, as they may be fairly called"; Tertullian, *Anti-Nicene Fathers*, vol. III, "A Treatise on the Soul", chapter 3, trans. by Peter Holmes.)

Lecture III – On Antithesis as a Method of Social Psychology

a close. And so philosophy set the agendas for the councils; with its antitheses, it pointed to areas where theology had to set the boundaries of its individual doctrines.

Among modern factions, many studies of oriental languages, histories and monuments would never have been undertaken, if the rival churches had not hoped to be able to confound their adversaries with them. The greater the care taken in Rome to reserve and limit the reading of the holy texts, the greater the zeal had to be in other places to propagate them. And so, as a result of these prohibitions and the opposition to them, there is no book in the world that has been made available in so many living languages. In many barbarian languages, it is still the first and only book available. The Koran, by contrast, as it is not proscribed to the people, can be read safely in one language only.

As soon as a nation acquires self-consciousness through its literature, that nation positions itself in antithesis to all powers that would aspire to dominate it. These powers then arm themselves with some other idea; they try to give it a different self-consciousness. Thus the Austrian says to Italy that it is a geographical expression; that it is merely a form impressed on a strip of land surrounded by mountains and sea: a *lusus naturae*.[26] Thus the Frenchman tells Italy it is a Latin nation, that it must remain firmly attached to the great empire; which, by seizing the two Isthmuses, will save the globe from the Anglo-Saxons' and Slavs' ambitions. Thus the Pope tells her she is the prebend of mankind. Individual interests translate to so many other, hostile doctrines. Against which, the embattled nation, iron and bronze being of no use to it for this purpose, is forced to create for itself, in a vast *antithesis*, a higher order of defence which extends even to those most abstruse forms of erudition that miserly narrow learning despises. Knowledge is power!

You see, gentlemen, the breadth of my argument: I cannot exhaust it here: it could dictate an entire work from others; from myself, merely a brief chapter; I confine myself to stating a principle.

Antithesis will therefore be one of the most necessary arguments in a *Psychology of Associated Minds*, which would have to precede the *Ideology of society*.

---

[26] Translator's note: "Freak of nature".

LECTURE IV
On Sensation in Associated Minds

Notes

The lecture on sensation was delivered by Cattaneo on Thursday, 15 December 1864.

However, the publishing history of this lecture is complex. Firstly, sensation was the subject of one of the lessons given at the high school in Lugano, and also one of the lectures delivered to the Institute in Milan; secondly, there was also a separate appendix to the high school lesson on sensation, specifically on sensation in associated minds, as the exercise books of Cattaneo's students show.[1]

A summary of the lecture was published in RENDICONTI IL I (1864), pp. 182-85; whereas OEI contains the following: *Sensation*, the text of the high school psychology lesson, and *On Sensation in Associated Minds* as an *Appendix* to the lesson.[2] The lecture itself was not published in OEI as part of the lectures on the *Psychology of Associated Minds*. Ghisleri, in FFC, published the summary of

---

[1] The exercise books of Cajo Grano Curti and Curzio Curti are held in ACM, cart. 17, pl. VII. On the first page inside the front cover of the former's exercise book we read as follows: "Philosophy, Cajo Grano Curti, as explained by Prof. Carlo Cattaneo, school year 1864-65"; on p. 157 it says: "Appendix. On sensation in associated minds", the text itself starts with the words "All schools" and is divided into eleven sections; Curzio Curti's exercise book, meanwhile, is consistent with the former.

[2] In OEI, vol. VII, p. 105, note 1, it says that the mss of the psychology lessons bear the date 1857; while in the introductory remarks to the readers ("Ai Lettori", OEI, vol. VI, p. 1, note 1), the editor states that the "manuscripts for the unpublished works contained in this volume comprise the summaries and notes used by Cattaneo to dictate his lessons, as well as the summaries of the same lessons made by several of his pupils at the high school in Lugano, some of which bear the teacher's approval". Bobbio was critical of the inaccuracies contained in this note (SF, I,

the lecture on sensation as part of the lectures on the psychology of associated minds, using the version in *RENDICONTI IL*, whereas Bobbio added the appendix to the high school lesson, thus bringing it within the remit of the lectures on associated minds (*SF*, I); the versions published in *OEI* and *SF* differ only slightly and apart from a few minor variants correspond to the summary published in the *Rendiconti*.

For the text of the critical edition which I curated in 2016, I used a transcription which I made myself of a manuscript that purports to contain the complete text of the lecture. The title indeed says as much: "Lecture to the Institute, *On Sensation,* Fragment of *a Psychology of associated Minds*" (*ACM*, cart. 15, pl. I). Although there are corrections, it looks like a final copy; a note on page 10 refers to a sheet which is part of another manuscript with the same archive catalogue number and the title: "*On Associated Minds or Second Psychology,* July 1855, Chapter I. *On Sensation*".

Both the date of this part of the manuscript and the textual source demonstrate the close link between lessons and lectures.

---

p. LXV). There is therefore no precise indication in *OEI* of the source from which the appendix on sensation in associated minds was taken.

Figure 6 On Sensation, Fragment of a Psychology of Associated Minds, manuscript's first page.

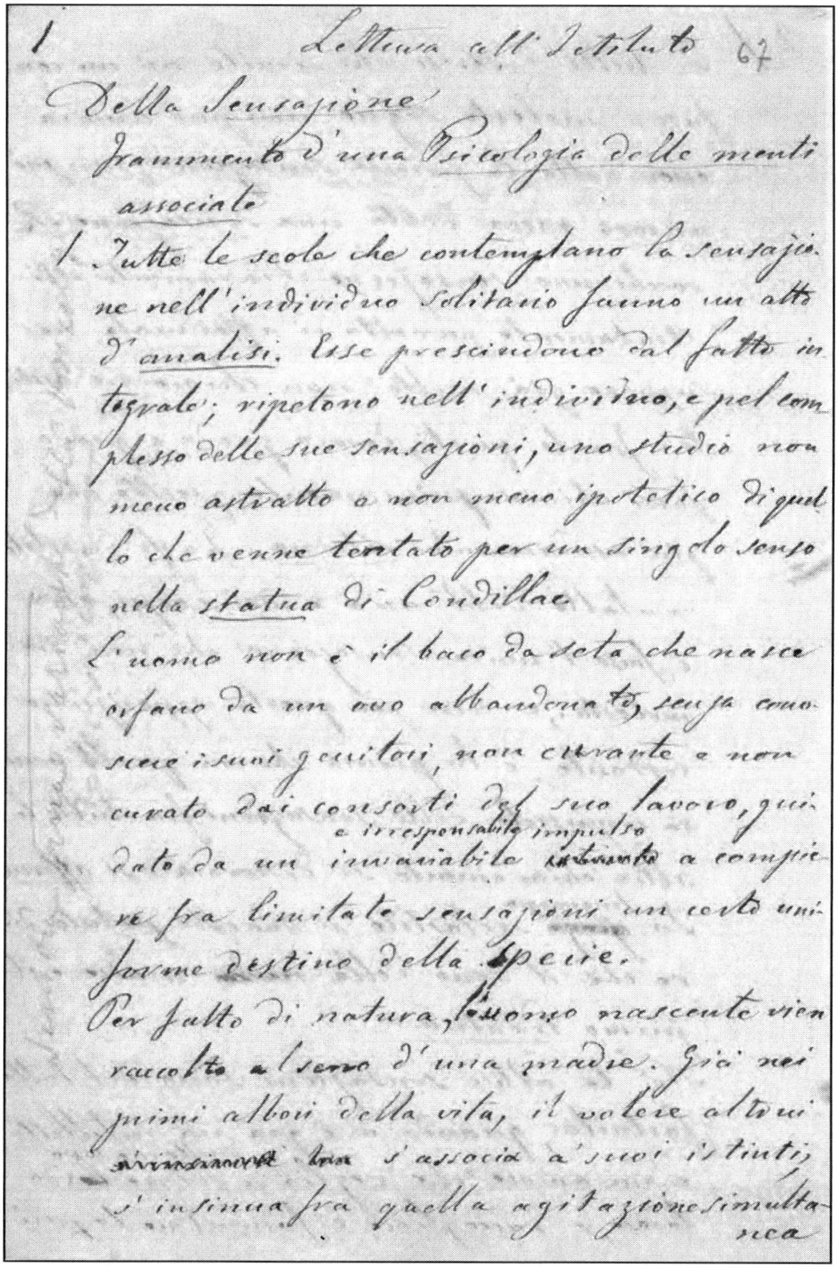

Lettera all'Istituto

Della Sensazione

Frammento d'una Psicologia delle menti associate

1. Tutte le scole che contemplano la sensazione nell'individuo solitario fanno un atto d'analisi. Esse prescindono dal fatto integrale; ripetono nell'individuo, e pel complesso delle sue sensazioni, uno studio non meno astratto e non meno ipotetico di quello che venne tentato per un singolo senso nella statua di Condillac.

L'uomo non è il baco da seta che nasce orfano da un ovo abbandonato, senza conoscere i suoi genitori, non curante e non curato dai consorti del suo lavoro, qui dato da un invariabile e irresponsabile impulso a compiere fra limitate sensazioni un certo uniforme destino della specie.

Per fatto di natura, l'uomo nascente vien raccolto al seno d'una madre. Già nei primi albori della vita, il volere altrui s'associa a'suoi istinti; s'insinua fra quella agitazione simultanea

Copyright Comune di Milano – all rights reserved – Milano, Palazzo Moriggia | Museo del Risorgimento

On Sensation

1. All schools of thought that contemplate sensation in the solitary individual engage in an act of *analysis*. But what they do not do is look at the whole picture: in the individual, and the entirety of his sensations, they effectively replicate an experiment that is no less abstract or hypothetical than the one attempted in the single senses of Condillac's *statue*.

Man is no silkworm, born an orphan from an abandoned egg without knowing its parents, not caring for, or cared for by, its working partners, guided by an invariable and irresponsible impulse to fulfil, amid limited sensations, a certain uniform destiny of the species.

It is a fact of nature that the new-born baby is gathered to its mother's breast. Right from the first signs of life, the will of others is associated with its instincts; it insinuates itself into that confused agitation of all the senses, which, like a confused and unhappy dream, cannot yet be said to be its *first sensation*, or even to be a *sensation* of any kind. For a sensation clearly and distinctly perceived and *affirmed* presupposes many other unclear and indistinct sensations: among which, the one that *recurs* most frequently is the first to gradually become clear. Among the unusual contacts with the air and foreign bodies, it is perhaps the only sensation that is not disagreeable; and, perhaps as a result of this continual contrast, is the first in that dark twilight of sensations amid all the others to be clearly discerned and to *affirm itself*. In scholastic language one would have said that the mother's breast is the first *identical*.[3]

---

[3] The bond between mother and child was an issue to which Cattaneo returned on many occasions. See, for example, the following comment: "Instinct binds the child to the mother through affectionate exchanges. Of all living creatures, man is the one that requires the longest period of nurturing; to meet this need, maternal love lasts longer in the human species than in

Lecture IV – On Sensation in Associated Minds

Nor are all the other sensations entirely casual, when there is already an intelligence and will at work which are minded to deflect the most painful of them and gather and foster only the most pleasant. Many sensations are common to all, because they are inevitable. But unfortunately it is fact that an infant's set of sensations already decides his pains and comfort, his screams and his sleep, and often his life and death. Statistics and medicine can tell philosophy how much greater the probability of pain, crying and death in childbirth is for mothers who are savages or who live in poverty. The set of initial sensations is already the work of several associated beings. Besides the instincts of the infant and its mother, there are the affections and customs of the family, and hence of the social institutions. Above all there is the mother's voice, which, in diligently accompanying the individual sensations, helps to fix and perceive them; it activates the attention without which sensation would simply flow, leaving no trace; and associates the individual sensations with a sound, a word, that becomes an indelible and distinctive sign, as though the fulfilment and seal of clear, distinct perception. Not just in these early moments but throughout life, the individual's sensations are always more or less dominated and, I would say, created, by the conditions of the society in which they live. Sensation in human beings is therefore not an unmediated encounter between the subject and various objects; it is not a *pure* fact; it is, right from its very beginnings, a social act.

A person who was born blind, or a deaf and dumb person, who did not take their first breaths in a society already enlightened by philosophy would not have been able to compensate for the missing sense's functions by replacing it with those of another.[4] In the man born blind who reads words with his finger, or in the deaf and dumb man who lip-reads them, an artificial sensation, which is by definition a late, social invention, supplies what is lacking in the natural sensation. In not too distant times, even in Europe deaf and dumb people were considered to be incapable of reason; they were drowned in the water or thrown to the animals, which is how the majority of mankind still treats them.

---

any other. Thus it forms the basis for domestic society and hence for every other form of society" (Swiss psychology lesson "Dell'instinto", *SF*, II, p. 131).

[4] The issue of instruction and education of blind, deaf and dumb people was discussed in *Il Politecnico*; cf. G. Polli, "Sul modo d'ammaestrare i sordomuti nella pronuncia orale; alcuni tentativi del dottor Giovanni Polli" (1839, II. 11, pp. 385-402); and A. Trinchinetti, "Sul potere dei sensi e della mente nei ciechi, e sugli stabilimenti destinati alla loro istruzione" (1839, II. 9, pp. 225-50). Drafts of the two articles are found in *ACM*, cart. 36, pl. II. On Trinchinetti's experiment on how people born blind who regain their sight as adults perceive objects, cf. Mazzarello, (*ILASL-II*, p. 593).

2. The individual does not always notice everything that surrounds him. Often he does not see and hear what another individual in the same place hears and sees. Age, gender, health, hunger, all instincts, all habits are coefficients without which the presence of objects on their own would be unable to bring about sensation. These motives often have their roots in the individual character, but more often in the modifications which society imprints on them. A naturalist who goes through a forest will carry with him the distinct impression of every plant and rock on which his gaze has dwelt, whereas the savage will notice only what is of use to the limited needs of his own life. If it is true that sensation precedes the idea, it is equally true that once the idea has been created, it is the latter idea that must determine new orders of sensation.

3. Let us suppose that a savage should come to have a distinct perception of all objects that surround him. His sensations will always be limited by his native country's horizon: a few species of plants for food, medicine or poisons; a few animals; the banks of a river, or a solitary sea; the hovels which shelter his unclothed tribe. When we think of the most remote parts of the earth, our imagination crowds with everything that is strange or unknown to us, as though we were in a botanical or zoological garden. It is the same the whole world over. But every region has its own aspect: one has an arid climate, another a rainy one; marshy lowlands or towering Alps; few families of plants cover hundreds of miles with a marvellous aspect for those who arrive there for the first time, but a uniform and tedious aspect to those who remain there. In the region where we live, which is one of the most pleasant and abundant in terms of vegetation, a good *fifth* of the flowering plants, more than five hundred species, belong to only two families of composites and grasses; many of them can barely be distinguished from each other even with careful study. As many as forty species of clover; for the botanist these will be different sensations; but for the unknowing *child of nature*, everything leaves but a single sensation.

Before the civilized *child of society*, all lands and oceans, archipelagos and deserts, volcanoes and glaciers reveal themselves in their variety. The animals of the opposite hemispheres are drawn and coloured in his books, conserved in his museums, living and self-moving in his gardens. This treasure trove of sensations is a gift which nature gives us by the hand of society.

4. And society not only sees things, but *makes them*. It transforms the earth into metals, dyes wools and silks different colours; with tender care, it creates innumerable varieties of flowers, fruits and domesticated animals; it transforms the woodlands into fields, changes the face of the earth, and erects the most

sublime architecture. We do not notice, but both bread and wine and the innumerable combinations of foods and aromas are gifts which nature similarly offers us by the hand of society. And when we consider musical instruments and the infinite combinations of sounds and tempos and the strong and sweet emotions with which life is comforted and delighted, the genius of society may well pride itself in comparison with the rare and poor harmonies of savage nature.

5. There is a world invisible to the barbarians but revealed to us by telescope and microscope. Once the telescope had been discovered, a whole host of phenomena became new sensations to the newly-equipped eye: the phases of Venus, the mountains on the moon, the moons of Jupiter, the ring of Saturn, the rotations of the sun's surface, the countless points of light which make up the Milky Way, the multiple star systems and nebulae. Once the microscope had been discovered, the infinite small particles that exist in a grain of clay, which move in a drop of water, which swim in the eye's humours, became new sensations for us. All chemistry is a revelation of previously invisible phenomena; no-one would have imagined that water could give rise to an invisible substance that can burn through iron and diamond, or a substance that is capable of raising us to the point where, in the higher reaches of the atmosphere, we encounter the sensation of ice, which the first illusion of our senses had caused us to think were scattered with fires.

And electrical equipment is for us like new senses, with which we can perceive sensations inaccessible to those instruments that nature alone gave us. With them, we may enter into conversation with those powers whose presence in the universe man in nature does not perceive. It is perfectly legitimate to imagine that, as by nature we have a sense which picks up vibrations of light, and a sense that detects sound waves, so too we might have been born with other instruments that could reveal magnetic influences to us, as the compass does. Those who gave us the magnetic needle to accompany us through the mists of the seas, the sandstorms of the desert and the labyrinths of the mines, who extended electrical telegraph wires from one slope of the mountainside to another, from one shore of the oceans to another, in so doing provided us with the *equivalent of a new* sense, as useful and real as the senses of sight and sound. It is of little relevance to the effect if an organ is materially inserted into our persons, or if the new phenomena, representing themselves spatially through the vibrations of a needle or a handset, translate to the sense of sight. Through it, our mind became initiated into an order of ideas that sight on its own was unable to give us and which, more than any other, is immersed in the universe's secrets.

6. The few sensations of the savage are sterile to the intellect, for they are vague, uncertain and immeasurable. He is unable to compare the heat of two summers, the cold of two winters. We, with our instruments, can determine, before our mind is able to, how much the cold varies from frost to frost, how much heat differs from fire to fire; we know at precisely what heat lead, and at precisely what heat iron, melts and becomes liquid; how many calories have to be accumulated in a season in order for a bunch of grapes to ripen.

7. Hitherto we have seen the phenomena of sensation multiply within society; however, each of them remains the object of individual perception. Now, there are phenomena which one individual alone could never perceive in their fullness, not even with the help of instruments; the senses of the many have to be associated with it. The men who saw Halley's comet return after almost a century were no longer the same as the ones who had admired its arrival. To conceive of the vastness of an earthquake, several men have to advise each other that they have felt shocks in distant regions at the same time. Observers scattered in various stations who are exploring the earth's magnetic tension and the course of the winds and the rains are the parts of the civilized nations' *common sensorium*.

8. To summarize, then, we may say that the association of minds allows them to: 1. Scour the world further, or to collect its scattered objects in greater number; 2. Produce new objects and new sensations by their own efforts; 3. Make things which are hidden to our senses artificially capable of being perceived sensorily; 4. Distinguish and measure degrees of sensation that cannot naturally be distinguished or measured; 5. Finally, truly associate the senses of several men in different points of time and space, so as to embrace certain phenomena in their wholeness that exceed the capacity of individual sense, out of which, from a crowd of uncertain and occasionally contradictory sensations, a stable and serene light gradually emerges to represent the order of the universe.

LECTURES V AND VI
On Analysis in Associated Minds

Notes

Two separate *lectures* were devoted to the subject of *Analysis*: the first of these, Analysis part I, delivered on 28 December 1865 in the *Class of Mathematical and Natural Sciences*, was Cattaneo's fifth *lecture* to the Institute; while Analysis part II, which in the past was thought to be the fifth lecture, was delivered on 16 August 1866, at the assembly of the *Class of Letters and Moral and Political Sciences*, and was the sixth and final lecture. (The Institute was and still is divided into the *Class of Letters and Moral and Political Sciences* and the *Class of Mathematical and Natural Sciences*.)

For Analysis part I, my reconstruction of events is as follows. On 14 December 1865 a meeting of the *Class of Letters and Moral and Political Sciences* was held. Some of Cattaneo's letters suggest he had been planning to deliver his lecture on analysis in November but was indisposed, so suggested 14 December as a date instead. Notice to such effect is found in his letter to the Institute's President's office:

> Having now recovered from a bout of serious rheumatic affections which prevented me from giving a Lecture at the first meeting in November, I expect to be able to deliver another part of my work on *Social psychology* on the 14th of this month, namely: *On Analysis as an operation of several associated minds, with application to the orders of Education.*[1]

---

[1] *EP*, IV, pp. 381-82, letter dated 6 December 1865; the same information is also repeated in another letter: "I had a very strong bout of rheumatism for several weeks, my wife was seriously ill; I was unable to leave the house […] I shall also write to the President's office that I think I will be able to deliver a Lecture on the 14th of this month.", *EP*, IV, p. 382, letter dated 6 December 1865, addressed to Mr Riganti.

Cattaneo was present at the meeting held on 14 December, but delivered the lecture on 28 December 1865 instead, at a meeting of the *Class of Mathematical and Natural Sciences*, as shown by the manuscript version of the minutes:

> Professor Cattaneo reads: On analysis as an operation of several associated minds with application to the orders of scientific education. An account of this lecture will be given by the Secretary to the Class of letters and moral and political sciences once the work has been completed.[2]

However, this account does not appear to exist, a fact which casts some doubt over the date of the lecture or whether it even took place.

The following year, on 5 August 1866, Cattaneo wrote again to the President's office: "If nothing untoward happens, I hope to take part in the assembly to be held on the 16th of this month and read the second part of an Essay: *On analysis* – as an operation of Associated Minds, with application to the orders of scientific education".[3] Thus it was only after Analysis part II (lecture VI) was given on 16 August 1866 that mention was made in RENDICONTI IL (III, 1866, p. 213) of a previous lecture by Cattaneo on the same subject.

In the brief space of time between the first and second lectures on analysis, the third Italian war of independence took place, with its fluctuating fortunes in which the Italian army and navy were defeated and Garibaldi and his volunteers alone were victorious.

After the lecture on 16 August 1866 Cattaneo wrote to his wife as follows:

> Anna dearest. I had an orange sorbet; which gave me some relief from the unbearable heat that has continued throughout the day. [...] It is half past nine now and I'm going to bed. You see what an orderly and exemplary person I become when I am far away from you. You are the reason for all my bad habits when I am near you, and all my virtuous ones when I am far away. And with all my bad habits and virtues, I fondly bid you farewell.[4]

---

[2] RENDICONTI IL, *Classe di Scienze matematiche e naturali*, II, 1865, 331, and minutes of meeting held on 28 December 1865, approved on 22 February 1866 (AIL, papers of the minutes of meetings, Bb 16, 41). RENDICONTI IL show that Cattaneo attended on both 14 and 28 December 1865.

[3] Two drafts of the letter are held in ACM, cart. 3, pl. XXVI; the title given in the other draft is: "*On Analysis* – Fragment of a *Psychology of Associated Minds*", and the phrase "with application to the orders of scientific education" has been crossed out.

[4] EP, IV, p. 422, letter dated 19 August 1866 to Cattaneo's wife (from SPE, III, p. 181, p. 182).

Lectures V and VI – On Analysis in Associated Minds

While still in Milan he completed an abstract for the Institute, much shorter than the lectures themselves, for inclusion in *Rendiconti IL* (*Classe di Lettere e Scienze morali e politiche*, III, 1866, pp. 213-15).

For many years the lecture on Analysis part I remained undated, and indeed the texts of the two lectures were never properly identified. In OEI (vol. VI) a single text was published, derived from two manuscripts held in ACM (cart. 15, pl. III), ascribed to two lectures combined sequentially and identified as numbers 1 and 2.[5] Ghisleri, starting from the text given in OEI, confirmed there had been two lectures on analysis, and dated the second precisely: 16 August 1866 (FFC, pp. 275-98). Bobbio reproduced the same combined text from OEI (SF, I, pp. 451-79).

In this edition, the texts reproduced and translated are, for lecture V, "On Analysis in Associated Minds. (Second draft)", which provides an introduction to the subject; and for lecture VI, "On Analysis in Associated Minds 2nd part", which begins as follows: "I interrupted my lecture by saying that free analysis is one of the greatest material and moral interests of mankind".

The first five paragraphs of the second manuscript are almost entirely identical to the abstract of the lecture included in *Rendiconti IL* (III, 1866, p. 213), but were not included in OEI or in any of the subsequent editions based on it. One reason for this exclusion might be that these paragraphs contain a reference to lecture V, which at the time had not been identified.

The unpublished Analysis part I (lecture V) has been identified by Fugazza as the manuscript entitled "On Analysis in Associated Minds. Read to the Institute on Dec.[ember] 1865" (ACM, cart. 15, pl. III) which she published along with other previously unedited writings by Cattaneo in "Filosofia e scienze umane: intorno ad alcuni autografi di Cattaneo" (Fugazza, 2005, pp. 239-44).

In his preparations for the lectures Cattaneo studied analysis in many of its various scientific applications. ACM (cart. 15, pl. II) contains excerpts from works and entries from the *Encyclopédie Nouvelle* transcribed by Cattaneo on subjects such as logical analysis and synthesis (Condillac), mathematical analysis (Abel Transon[6]), analytical mechanics (Lagrange[7]), and chemical analysis.

The first of the two lectures presents itself as an introduction to his research: "My intention is to speak of those great analyses that were performed by consensus, often unobserved and sometimes involuntarily, between several minds

---

[5] A note in OEI states that: "Despite the research carried out it has not been possible to establish the date of this lecture, or the one on the same subject that followed it, which has been transcribed here from the Author's own manuscripts" (p. 274).

[6] Abel Étienne Louis Transon (1805-76).

[7] Giuseppe Luigi Lagrange (1736-1813).

associated in a common work" of human kind; this is followed by an illustration of what analysis is and how it should be done: namely in continued, orderly, exhaustive and above all free fashion. The second part studies the formation of human knowledge by means of a historical survey, with a particular focus on scientific thought, before concluding with some proposals as to how university teaching should be organized.

The following texts are published here, both of which based on the transcriptions contained in *PMA-EC*, 2016:

- Lecture V part I, "On Analysis in Associated Minds (Second draft)", undated;
- Lecture VI part II, "On Analysis in Associated Minds. Part 2", undated.

Figure 7 On Analysis in Associated Minds. Part I, manuscript's first page.

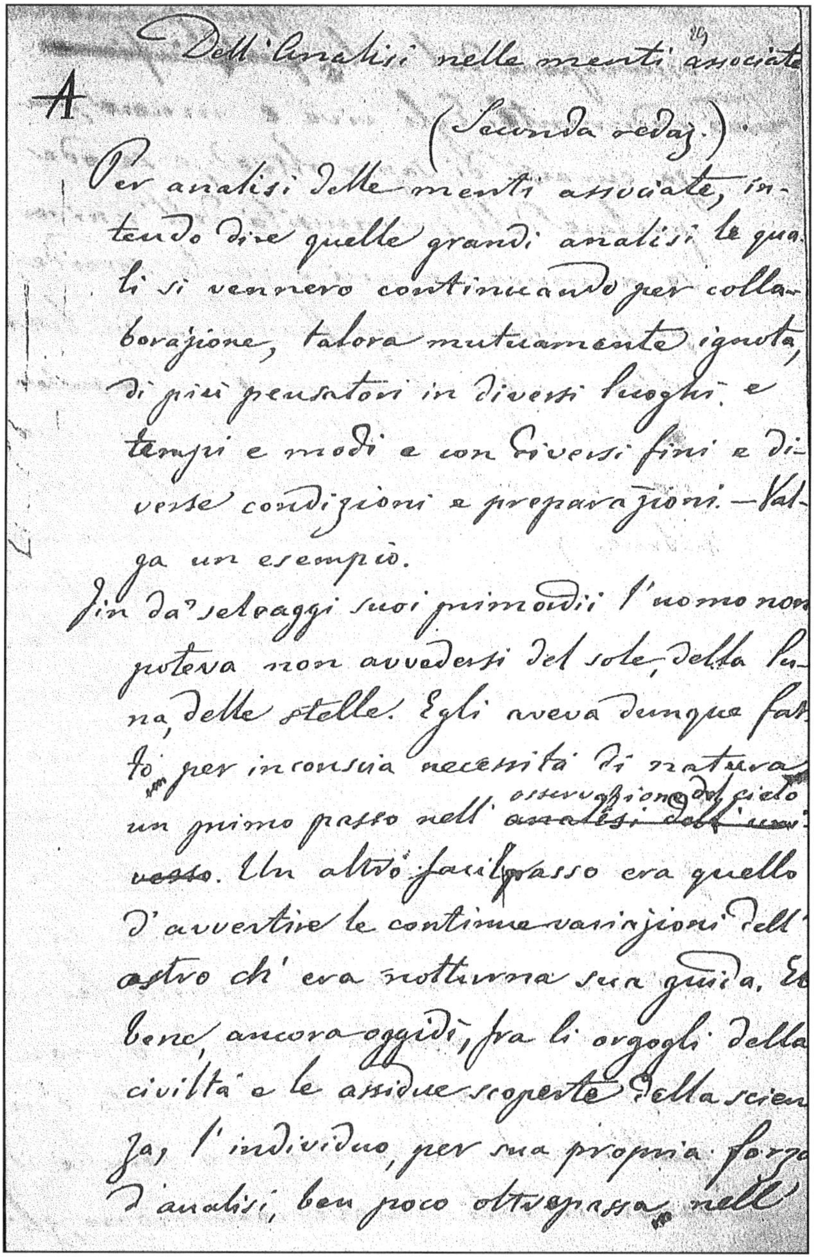

Copyright Comune di Milano – all rights reserved – Milano, Palazzo Moriggia | Museo del Risorgimento

Lecture V
On Analysis in Associated Minds
Part 1

What I mean by analysis of associated minds is those great analyses which were carried on by means of a collaboration, sometimes mutually unawares, between various thinkers in different places and times and means and with different purposes and different conditions and preparations. – Let us take an example.

From his earliest savage origins, man could not help but notice the sun, moon and stars. In this way, by unconscious necessity of nature, he took a first step in the observation of the heavens. Another easy step was to notice the continual changes in the star which served as his nocturnal guide. Now, even today, despite civilization's achievements and science's diligent discoveries, the individual alone, by the force of his own analysis, barely gets beyond those first rudiments in the observation of the heavens. He lives and dies without caring to know more; and if he hears talk of the immensity of the universe, admires it; more often than not smiles, as though listening to a fairy tale; and soon forgets it. Such are the limits of mental activity in the individual, it matters little whether civilized or savage.

Now, when we read in the astronomy books that science today has reached the point where it is able to distinguish a whole host of shining suns within a solitary star, we must recognize that the person who verifies this wonder with their telescope is, in effect, performing a *simple act of analysis*, as they were when, with the naked eye, they saw them as though confused in a single light. Whether the eye is so empowered or not, the act which is proper to the intellect in that moment is the same, even though the sense itself, in such changed conditions, announces the presence of several points of light in that star rather than just one. Analysis is still analysis; it is still *an act with which the mind distinguishes the parts of a whole*. But the eye could never have come to be so em-

Lecture V – On Analysis in Associated Minds – Part 1

powered and guided, without the slow preparation of social life. That act is the final result of the work of forefathers and heirs; the work of several, associated generations.

To begin with, the alternation of sun and moon must create an illusion in the imagination that there are two bodies, differing from earth only slightly in terms of size and distance, and each bright shining with its own light, at the service of the earth's *motionless plain*, amid a multitude of minute stars, scattered in an azure vault sitting above the highest of mountains. But as social analysis continually progresses, this azure vault becomes a limitless space, those minute sparks become an infinite number of suns; around the nearest of which the humble *globe* of the earth *moves*, bringing with it, by virtue of a nearer attraction, the even smaller globe of the moon which reflects a light not its own.

Here the primitive analysis, always accessible to each *individual*, seems in conflict with the later ones carried out over the course of the centuries, first among certain nations and then others, by means of work that is *social* in nature, which has often slowed in those same nations and in some cases is now derelict.

The laws of analytical force are thus not to be sought only in those of the intellect. *Perception of truth is part of the nations' destiny.*

Unfortunately, among the various peoples, the *exercise of analysis is preordained and the result of fate*. Even today peoples live in the presence of countless phenomena of nature and society, without ever having been able to direct their attention to observing them, and almost without seeing them: – indeed, often without *wanting* to see them.

Not so many as three centuries have passed since, through the light shone by anatomical analysis, man finally realized that blood circulates in his veins. Not so much as a single century has passed since, through the light shone by chemical analysis, he first found out what the vital element was of the air which he breathes. It is only in our days, in comparative linguistic analysis, that he has been able to distinguish the long forgotten blending of nations; and in analysis of fossils, that he finally saw the indelible chronologies of the earth and man.

It is one thing to explain how those *discoveries* were not made many centuries earlier; it is another thing to explain how the *research* that eventually led to them being made was not carried out many centuries earlier. Research was not free; so the intellect could do nothing. Many things were inaccessible; many things for a long time seemed pointless to know; many things seemed wicked and evil; they were prohibited by the powerful, and even by the wise. In the most sublime developments of the intellect, the will exerts greater dominion than the intellect itself does.

The modus operandi of analysis, neglected by and virtually unknown to ancient philosophy, was studied deliberately by modern psychology; but only according to the Cartesian hypothesis of the *individual*. Now, this hypothesis does not take into consideration the fact that mankind is, by its primitive and spontaneous nature, gregarious and social; and that *the most social and gregarious act of man is thought*, for often it brings together many people unknown even to each other, and many generations, in a single thought. Nor does it consider how or from where, in that instinctive and spontaneous association of minds, analysis is able to draw on a more noble initiative, – nor how it first expands, then restricts, its free activity. But given that this faculty must be considered as *essential to the intellect*, it is worth studying how, *nonetheless*, free analysis has to date been unable to be *performed by the whole of humankind*. It is worth studying how among many peoples, following rapid emancipation, analytical forces became enslaved again; – how no nation to date has been able to keep the course of its thoughts continually alive and free; – how many nations have disappeared, like meteors, without leaving the legacy of an idea; – how every society, without realizing, sets its own limits on the sphere of its analysis; – how we ourselves, who are gathered here in the name of living science, are not all yet able, released as we are from every precedent of our own or of others, to stretch out our hand to reach all branches of the scientific tree equally. Free analysis is one of the great moral and material interests of human kind.

Philosophy should therefore set itself a fundamental subject for study: – *the analysis of free analysis.*

Let us briefly consider analysis per se, as it proceeds in the *individual* and *associated minds*. When Hernan Cortes[8] first arrived in Mexico, the ancient inhabitants were overcome and terrorized by Spanish horsemanship, to the point where, in their turmoil, wonder and fear, they thought horse and rider were the same animal. It is the ancient fable of the centaurs; it is sudden, indistinct sensation, exaggerated by the imagination. To begin with, even the tranquil sight of a wood or clear sky, brings the perception of almost a *single object*, – a broad expanse of vegetation, – a swathe of sparkling azure sky. But the person who then focuses their attention on some of the plants and stars, obtains other evidence that gradually clarifies the initial concept.

Continued analysis therefore tends to scrutinize, even in several attempts, the *whole* of each thing; – and not to disunite, dissolve or "*resolve*", as the term *analysis* has led many thinkers to suppose. "*Armé de l'analyse, il désunira*", said

---

[8] Hernan Cortes (1485-1547).

Lecture V – On Analysis in Associated Minds – Part 1

Pierre Leroux.[9] But to number the fingers on the hand or the distinctive parts of a flower is not to disunite them; rather, it is to unite them forever, in the concept of number. It was with Linnaeus's numerical analysis that botany first became a science. Anatomy, while separating bones, joints, muscles, nerves, arteries and veins (for the material necessity of being able to see them), contemplates them as things that are joined to each other, and insofar as, and how, they are inter-related; in fact, it sheds light on hitherto unknown links between them. When it observes that the four smaller fingers bend in opposition to the base of the thumb, it discerns how the hand has the ability to take hold of things and to squeeze them. The unexpected discovery of the *Eustachian tube*, a canal which connects the intimate cavity of the mouth with that of the ear, reveals how a person who listens open-mouthed, increases the effectiveness of their hearing unawares.

The same occurs when analysis has that abstract and universal appearance given by algebraic formulae, because this common appearance makes even those concepts which at first sight appear to have no clear connection, comparable to, and commutative with, each other. Thus the mind is able to discern what is identical, constant, essential and certain in the confusion of what appears on the surface to be different.

Ordered analysis proceeds from the most obvious and evident things to the most abstruse; wherein resides the principle of every demonstration and instruction.

Analysis may be said to be complete when it extends, to a given equal degree of depth, to a given entire field of observation; that is, to a given *being* or *phenomenon* or *set* of being or phenomena and to all of their *parts*, *qualities* and *relations*, within the limit and according to the purpose which the observer has set themselves. Analysis of soils which is sufficient for a manufacturer of roof tiles is not sufficient for a manufacturer of porcelain china. And analysis can always return to work later; it can gather a further series of perceptions in the same field. There are no limits that can be assigned to it, absolutely or universally.

But even in the narrowest circle, given that the analysis cannot comprehend everything in equal depth, the parts which are observed remain confused with those that have been neglected or are inaccessible. To fill this gap, the imag-

---

[9] Cattaneo's note: "*Encycl. nouv. – Analyse.*". Probably a reference to the *Encyclopédie Nouvelle* by Pierre Leroux and Jean Reynaud, published in eight volumes (1835-41). The following volume was also part of Cattaneo's library: *De l'Humanitè, de son principe, et de son avenir, ou se trouve exposèe la vrai definition de la religion et ou l'on explique le sens, la suite, et l'enchaînement du mosaisme, et du christianisme, par Pierre Leroux* (Paris: Perrotin, 1840), 2 vols (*BC*, n. 962).

ination floods in with its thousands of ghosts. From that point on, in all the intellect's subsequent deliberations, what is true becomes enmeshed with what is false, until the work of exhaustive and faithful analysis is resumed by posterity. Thus in primitive science, the audacious flights of fancy outweigh the slow pace of observation.

Now, analysis which is *evident, distinct in all of its parts, ordered and exhaustive*, meets the four rules of the Cartesian method. Which method is therefore no more than analysis. And yet the new Cartesians labour to identify it with synthesis. E B. Saint-Hilaire refused to speak of synthesis entirely, referring his readers simply to the method instead.[10] But whether synthesis or analysis is used, observance of the four rules would not lead to *l'indiscutable certitude*. When Descartes published the *Discours de la methode* in 1637, a few years before Galileo died, he had already been witness throughout his life to how everyone found *l'indiscutable certitude* and *la prodigieuse clarté* in the misleading evidence of the earth's motionlessness. But that motionlessness was an illusion; and the cause of the universal illusion was precisely that *evidence*![11]

Chemical analysis does not tend only to distinguish substances that manifest themselves spontaneously by their active properties; nor does it tend only to recognize the known substances in the bodies that conceal them; but it goes as far as discovering the unknown existence of those which nature itself never revealed, such as oxygen, calcium, chlorine and other principles diffused widely in the air, on the earth and in the sea.

However, we shall not say, with Leroux, that man, "*armed with analysis, will disunite*". With supreme evidence chemistry performs the demonstration of many analyses, even for acts of composition or recomposition, entirely devoid of all decomposition. A magnesium ribbon, placed on the scales in contact with a live flame, burns, rapidly increasing in weight and thus revealing the invisible oxygen it absorbs from the atmosphere. Here the recomposition of the two principles is the reverse demonstration and counterproof of what the analytical mind discovered directly; it is a means, not an end; there is no new discovery; there is no new idea. In practical terms it may be called a synthesis; in logical terms it is a *distinction*; it is the final complement of *distinction*.

For the most part, chemical substances do not leave one compound unless to join another; the more complicated procedures reduce to a series of transpositions and substitutions of this kind. – The substances change properties merely by varying in proportion; sweet mercury, a mild medicine used for chil-

---

[10] Jules Barthelemy-Saint-Hilaire (1805-95).
[11] Cattaneo's note: "*V. Dict. des sciences philos. – Méthode* p. 260, *Synthèse*.".

dren, with the addition of an equivalent amount of chlorine is transformed into a corrosive sublimate. – Countless organic combinations of carbon and water change properties only when they are arranged in a different order, – like rose and terebinth essential oils, both of which consist of precisely carbon and water in identical proportions, – and yet have such different appearances and properties. – Certain latent substances are manifested even only by being exposed to certain changes in temperature, humidity, electricity; the colour shows the vapours of iodine; the odour reveals the vapours of arsenic. – But in any such procedure of decomposition or composition or recomposition or transposition or substitution or apposition or disposition or exposition, the supreme office of analysis remains intact at all times, which is *distinction*!

Thinkers of an imaginative and fervid mind hate the slowness of analysis and its rigours and checks; they call it a pedestrian and material faculty: *ingenium in dorso*.[12] This is the ancient Brahminic, Buddhist, Eleatic, Platonic condemnation; always blind disdain, at times outright curses. But it is true that every most subtle abstraction is always the work of analysis. From the abstractions of numbers with no object, lines with no surfaces, surfaces without depth, forms without body, forces without substance, mathematics arises. From abstractions of solid and void, identical and different, self and non-self, being and non-being, infinite and absolute, logic, ontology and metaphysics arise. Everything that is most sublime in the intellect begins from the analytical act of abstraction. Abstraction becomes the common bond of all phenomena of science and conscience. Analysis is the pyramid of which synthesis is the pinnacle.

---

[12] Translator's note: "supine genius".

Figure 8 On Analysis in Associated Minds. Part II, manuscript's first page.

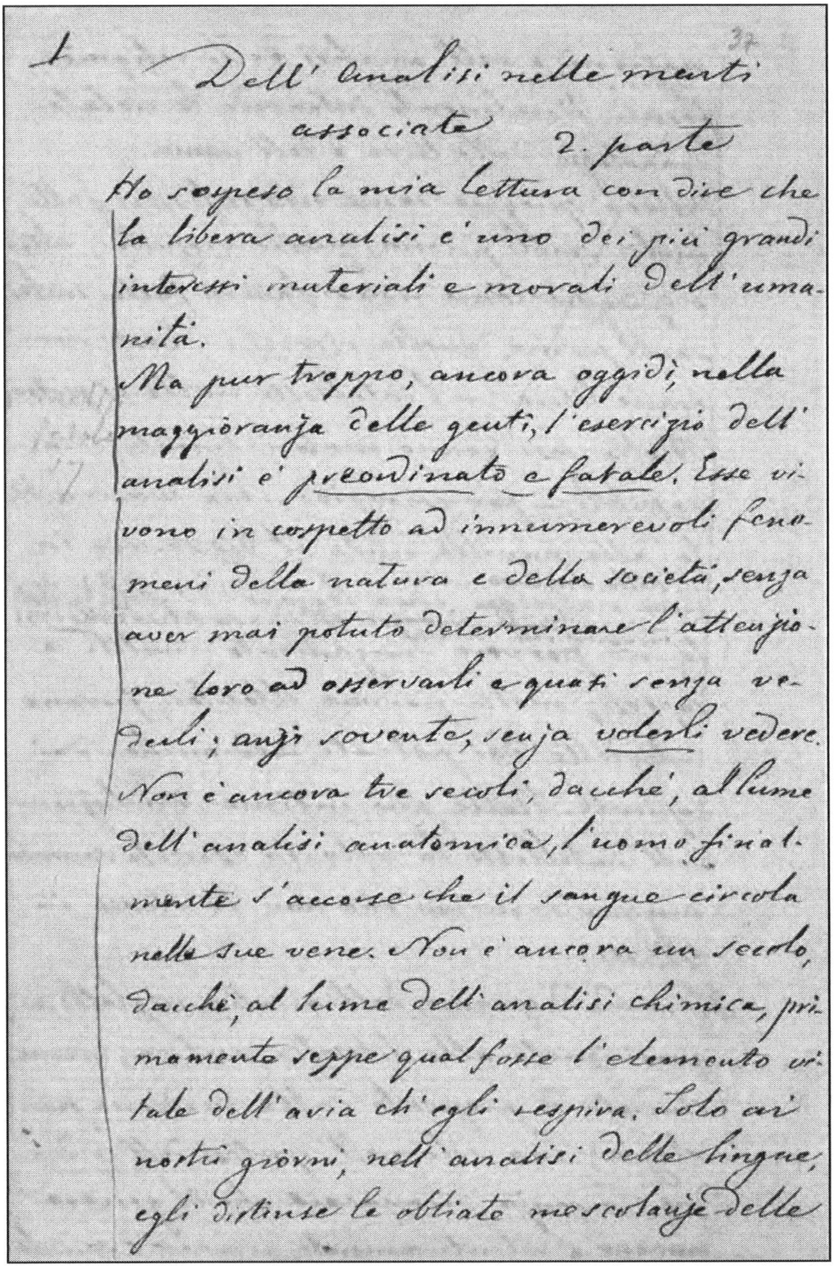

> Dell'analisi nelle menti associate 2. parte
>
> Ho sospeso la mia lettura con dire che la libera analisi è uno dei più grandi interessi materiali e morali dell'umanità.
>
> Ma pur troppo, ancora oggidì, nella maggioranza delle genti, l'esercizio dell'analisi è preordinato e fatale. Esse vivono in cospetto ad innumerevoli fenomeni della natura e della società, senza aver mai potuto determinare l'attenzione loro ad osservarli e quasi senza vederli; anzi sovente, senza volerli vedere. Non è ancora tre secoli, dacché, al lume dell'analisi anatomica, l'uomo finalmente s'accorse che il sangue circola nelle sue vene. Non è ancora un secolo, dacché, al lume dell'analisi chimica, pel primo momento seppe qual fosse l'elemento vitale dell'aria ch'egli respirava. Solo ai nostri giorni, nell'analisi delle lingue, egli distinse le obliate mescolanze delle

Copyright Comune di Milano – all rights reserved – Milano, Palazzo Moriggia | Museo del Risorgimento

LECTURE VI
On Analysis in Associated Minds
Part 2

I interrupted my lecture by saying that free analysis is one of the greatest material and moral interests of mankind.

Unfortunately, even today, among the majority of peoples the exercise of analysis is *preordained and the result of fate.* They live in the presence of countless phenomena of nature and society, without ever having been able to direct their attention to observing them, and almost without seeing them; indeed, often without *wanting* to see them. Not so many as three centuries have passed since, through the light shone by anatomical analysis, man finally realized that blood circulates in his veins. Not so much as a single century has passed since, through the light shone by chemical analysis, he first found out what the vital element of the air which he breathes was. It is only in our days, in comparative linguistic analysis, that he has been able to distinguish the forgotten blending of nations; and in analysis of fossils, that he has finally seen the indelible chronologies of the earth and man.

It is one thing to explain how those *discoveries* were not made many centuries earlier; it is another thing to explain how the *research* which eventually led to them being made was not carried out many centuries earlier. Research was not free; – so the intellect could do nothing. Many things were materially inaccessible; – for example: – the naked eye was unable to discern the legion of lights in a star or a nebula; from whence to arise to the synthetic idea of the universe's immensity. Many things for a long time seemed pointless to know; many things seemed unlawful; they were prohibited by the powerful; – and even by the wise. In the most sublime developments of the intellect, the *will* often exerts greater dominion than the *intellect* itself.

The *modus operandi* of analysis, neglected and virtually unknown to ancient philosophy, has been studied deliberately by modern psychology; but only according to the hypothesis of the *individual*; and without recognizing that mankind is instinctively gregarious and social more than any other living genus; – and without examining how, in natural society, analysis found the source of a nobler initiative; – nor how it first expanded, then contracted, its free activity.

But since we all consider this faculty to be *essential to the intellect*, so too we must propose to study how, *nonetheless*, free analysis has to date been unable *to be performed by the whole human race*. We must propose to study how, among many peoples following a rapid emancipation, analytical forces become enslaved again; – how *no* nation to date has been able to keep the course of its thoughts continually alive and free; how every society, without realizing, sets its own limits on the sphere of its analysis; how we ourselves, who are gathered here in the name of living and free science, are not all yet able, even released as we are from every precedent of our own or others, to stretch out our hand to reach all branches of the scientific tree equally.

Philosophy should therefore set itself a fundamental subject for study: – *the analysis of free analysis.*

When Descartes, with an act of pure and free analysis, distinguished *the conscience of being within the conscience of thought*, he was seeking, with this affirmation of the *self*, to be released from both *nature* and *society*. But nature had already gone before his intellect; but society had already given him the scientific tradition. That voice which to him seemed to have arisen solitarily from within his own conscience, was the first word of a problem that had already accumulated in the course of the centuries and the succession of philosophies: – a problem which the solitary *self* could not even have posed.

So it is. Both *nature* and *society* have a part in the development of analytical power. And as they are the causes that awaken it, so too they are the causes that can render it perpetually inert. I say "perpetually inert"; because in our memory, some peoples have become extinct or been confused with others or submerged into them, before, even after thousands of years, having surpassed with their own minds the extremely low limit that is granted even to the instinctive discernment of animals.

Nature had already established a disparity of conditions between one people and another, according to the disparity of useful or harmful things and of places and climates. The individual peoples, in their individual countries, were only able to notice what it had placed there. The presence of certain fruits which were obviously comestible, of certain animals which were tamer or wilder, the combination of land and climate, flora and fauna, thus imposed on the aboriginals *a series of acts of attention*, co-ordinated to the series of the most immediate necessities; and as *inevitable* there as they were impossible elsewhere.

Lecture VI – On Analysis in Associated Minds – Part 2

And so the aboriginals, in their individual native regions, had to constitute *the individual parts of a superficial analysis, fragmented and dispersed throughout the inhabited land*. The remaining nature lay unobserved and indistinct. For mankind it was though it did not exist.

As for *society*, however isolated and wretched it might have been, in its midst these individual fragments of observation had to survive the *individual*. What the infant learnt out of necessary coexistence and through blind imitation, must have seemed to him to be the necessary, and only possible, order of life. This is how *tradition* was born, – involuntary, spontaneous, un-reflexive, – but *imperious even then as it still is for us even now.* – Analysis was not free.

The individual was no longer obliged to begin the whole series of those discoveries over again on their own. Rather, each mind entered into the course of thought already marked by the thought of others. Analysis, born the servant of nature, grew as the servant of society.

Tradition was the tenacious thread that joined minds in association, not *from people to people*, but from *generation to generation*. It was the perpetual society of heirs with their forefathers. Even in the deepest recesses of minds, each generation was the daughter not only of its *territory* but also its *ancestors*. It was a direction given, and a restriction imposed, on the intellects of those still to be born, over a distance of centuries. Certain notions were already determined in the heart of the savage family, which had to survive to a later civilization. Many observances and aversions to foods and other family customs, which survive here and now among peoples, are traditions from time immemorial; originally perhaps they were mere admissions to, or omissions from, those primitive analyses.

To clarify the facts of their histories, the Romans used to refer back to what they called the origins, even though these were already interwoven with poetic fantasies. And equally, only from the origins is it possible to explain certain facts of the modern world. Let us take an example: – as late as the sixteenth century, in the splendid Mexico City, built with hydraulic artifice between two lakes, with fine rectilinear and rectangular thoroughfares, a ritual continuation of the cannibalistic way of life was still practised on top of the lofty pyramids, probably by this stage only to terrorize the subject peoples, and by way of statecraft.[13] But the origins of this atrocious idea, in a nation already rich in many trades and instructed in the priestly colleges, were the uninterrupted traditions of savage life.

---

[13] Cf. "Gli antichi messicani", *SSG*, III, pp. 97-129 (*Il Politecnico* IX. 1 (1860), 170-93); Cattaneo dealt with this issue at length in his Swiss lesson on ideology, in part III, "Ideologia delle genti" (VIII: "Della teocrazia militare del Messico", *SF*, III, pp. 65-77).

The intimate and common bond of all these primitive analyses is language. Discourse is one continuous analysis. It is necessary to analyse thought in order to translate it into words; by the same token, it is necessary to analyse words in order to be able to extract thought from them. Man, forced from childhood to follow the diligent comings and goings of that analytical process which modulates every concept of his own and others, giving them the prescribed social form, cannot entirely erase all traces of that perennial discipline to the point where they do not then survive, indelibly, in the subsequent additions to their language and in their blends and transformations between languages.

Let us take an example: – in numeration, the language of the Aztecs of Mexico mentioned above, proceeds not in multiples of ten but of five. It is clear that this must have originated from the primitive analysis of *one hand only.* And unfortunately, other Oceanic, American and African peoples survive in this century, who have never managed to develop their numerals, even to be able to count on the fingers of one hand. From childhood, they are accustomed to do without numbers, as their ancestors did for thousands of years. Hence *all their concepts, not just of number but also of space, time, measurement, distance, height, value, and force* are *indeterminate*; they are irreparably vague and vain. All their mental and material potential is neutered as a result. I believe that in the practice of trade, they will inevitably have to complete their numeration. But I also believe they will no longer be able to deduce any new numbers from the same principle from which they previously deduced the first; rather, they shall have to appropriate them straight from the European numbers, exactly as they are accustomed to hear them in the market place. This is what the Europeans themselves did, when they borrowed the term *million* from Italian; which, organically speaking, was born merely as an augmentative suffix, an inflected form that they did not have in their own languages.

When the individual peoples in their individual regions had established, *with their various initial analyses, an equivalent number of initial traditions, expressed in an equivalent number of linguistic rudiments*, they were able increase these initial resources in different ways. – They were able to notice other things around themselves, useful or harmful, hitherto unobserved. – They could, whether out of repeated attention, association of ideas or through an individual flash of genius, discern, in objects already familiar, new properties and new correspondences to common needs. It occurred, for example, that one of the wiser among those barbarians, finding themselves already instinctively armed with a piece of wood, as even an orangutan or a gorilla might do, could, by the strength of intellect which is proper to human beings, transcend that instinctive limit, and see in a sharp flint or the remains of a fish, an object with which to fashion a knife, an axe, a lance, or an arrow. – It occurred that one, in the terrible experience of a poison, saw a way to make those poor weapons more fearsome, and so set certain death upon both animals and enemies. – It occurred that someone, falling into a river, saved themselves purely instinctively by grabbing hold of a floating tree trunk; and in continuing and repeating this act, perceived the *main idea* of the art of shipping. In these new insights, the analytical action of the individual begins to *go beyond tradition and against tradition*. These were the *first efforts at free analysis*.

This power of the individual, who sees in things what others did not see, when it exalts itself to the highest level and finds a *main idea*, that is, the foundation for a new series of ideas, is what constitutes *genius*; for it is considered the work of an intelligence superior to human nature, and almost like that of a guardian spirit. The ancients considered all these main ideas of an art or science to be truly gifts to humanity from the gods or demi-gods.

But *chance* too played a large part in these new analyses. – It is said that the Phoenicians, in burning a mass of sea grass on the silica sands of the seashore, saw molten glass flow for the first time. It is also said that the Spanish discovered copious deposits of silver chloride in much the same way.

When individual action, or the action of fortuitous chance, intervenes, it is easy to explain how the nations were able to arrive at what might be a more abstruse idea, without being able to perceive what might be a more obvious one. Thus we see the heroes of the *Iliad* fighting aboard chariots and not yet mounted on horseback. Thus the use of guano appears to have been widespread in Peru, at a time when agriculture there was still carried out using wooden instruments. Thus in Australia, no-one for thousands of years conceived of even the most basic form of house or ship; yet there was someone who came up with the idea of obstructing the waters in the narrowest passages using stones and wood in order to imprison the fish there.

At this juncture, I may be permitted to note that many now believe it to have been demonstrated that in the chronology of the primitive nations, the wood, stone, copper and iron ages follow on from each other in fixed order. In the classical tradition, the gold age came first; and this might perhaps represent belief in a law of decadence rather than in one of progress. However, in America it is certain that at the time of the conquest, only the use of gold was widespread and ancient, whereas copper and iron were entirely unknown there. And it was gold in our memory that attracted the flood of emigration to California and Australia, where the aboriginals had not discovered any other metal. Science must take account of such varieties, and must not be too concerned to close the role of the facts, so that further analysis can remain free and so that the discoveries made and announced with unanimous testimonies do not appear to be contradicted by later discoveries.

Hitherto I have confined myself to the assumption of universally *isolated* traditions. But right from the origins, the discoveries can *spread* from tribe to tribe, short distances at least.

It was observed that around the pile dwellings on the lakes, where the savages of ancient Europe made their homes, cutting stones were gathered in certain places which they used to form knives and lances, when the use of metals was still unknown. But as the geologists noted that such stones were not naturally scattered in those vicinities, they deduced that they must have been brought there by a primitive version of communication of neighbours between other savages, friendly or hostile as the case may be, who may have found them elsewhere or have received them from others.

Hence these humble little stones would have been the oldest document not only of *commerce from people to people*, but the first *dissemination of an idea*. Minds hitherto associated only in the traditions of the *past* had thus already begun to communicate with each other, from tribe to tribe, the ideas of the *present*. *The dissemination of ideas between neighbours* was already being added to inherited tradition.

Similarly, when the ashes and charcoal of those savages' fires are uncovered in those sepulchral lands, we have an ancient document of the contemporary dissemination of fire; – another main idea, the most productive of all, and the most varied in its applications to the discovery of other main ideas. This new source of heat and light was also handed down to subsequent ages as a sacred object. In the Zend Avesta, the foundation of cities and colonies is called *the spread of fires*.[14] In even more distant centuries, the Persian kings used to send sacred fires before their armies, burning upon silver altars, as though with this gift they were wanting to entice the peoples to accept the goods of their rule: – *Ignis, quem ipsi sacrum et aeternum vocabant, argenteis altaribus praeferebatur* (Curt. 3.3. Forc., *Ignis*).[15]

Sacred fire was tended in the temples; if it went out, it was rekindled with mystical solemnity, the *tradition* of which continues among our changed belief. Participation in the fire always remained a right of the family, a right of the peo-

---

[14] The *Avesta* is a collection of religious texts of Zoroastrianism. The name *Zend-Avesta* was coined by French orientalistc Abraham Hyacinthe Anquetil Duperron (1731-1805); *Zend*, meaning interpretation, refers to the literature on the *Avesta* texts themselves.

[15] Egidio Forcellini, *Totius Latinitatis Lexicon, consilio et cura Jacobi Facciolati lucubratum, a Josepho Furlanetto auctum et emendatum* (Prati: Giachetti, 1839), entry *Ignis*; Cattaneo had a copy of the first part of this lexicon in three volumes in his library (*BC*, n. 658).

Lecture VI – On Analysis in Associated Minds – Part 2

ples; exclusion from the fire was an insult, a punishment, an exile, a war, a curse: – *Hostes judicemur; aquâ et igni nobis interdicatur* (D. Br. Forc. *Interdicere*).[16]

Gentlemen, humanity is but young. The invention of fire has barely circled the globe. I read in my early years, in the collection of La Harpe's works or Cook's travels,[17] if I remember correctly, that in some island of the great Ocean, when the aboriginals saw fire burning for the first time, they thought it was a living thing, and having dared to touch it, they believed themselves to have been bitten by a fierce animal. Here the dissemination between neighbours has expanded to become *dissemination between nations*. The observations of a tribe become the knowledge of human kind.

Every new *art* becomes a new field for analysis. The person who discovered fire paved the way for metals to be discovered. The person who saw a ship in a floating tree trunk, preordained for himself and his own, as he did for foreigners too, for the living but also for their successors, a series of successive discoveries, which, without limit in terms of matter or form, increasing the whole time, has reached us and will continue to grow for as long as humanity endures. But these successive analyses which the new arts bring forth from within a main idea involve observing the laws of *nature, in order to be conformed* to it: – "*Natura parendo vincitur*", – said Bacon.[18] And they prove to be easier, or more difficult, depending on whether they correspond to the traditions and dispositions of *societies*. The minds associated in this hereditary and progressive analysis therefore oscillate perpetually between an ideal which represents the invariable laws of *nature* and another ideal order that represents, in given times, places and peoples, the conditions of *society*.

All this progress of ideas remains beyond the hypothesis of the *thinking individual*; it goes as far beyond the *metaphysical solitude* of Descartes as it does beyond Condillac's *sensitive* statue, Rousseau's *poetic solitude*, and Vico's *common nature of nations*. To complete Vico's theory, it remains to be clarified how, if the nature of peoples is common, the colonies of the progressive nations in many parts of the earth find themselves faced with every degree of barbarian inertia. This is the greatest problem facing humanity. For it to be studied, its study must first be proposed.

---

[16] *Ibid.*, entry *Interdicere*.

[17] Jean François Laharpe (or La Harpe) (1739-1803); James Cook (1728-79).

[18] "Natura non nisi parendo vincitur ", from the *Novum Organum* by Francis Bacon, (1561-1626). (Translator's note: "Nature is conquered only by obedience"; Francis Bacon, "Aphorism III", *The New Organon*, ed. by Lisa Jardine and Michael Silverthorne (Cambridge: Cambridge University Press, 2000), p. 33.)

Going through the entire series of ideas we have reviewed this far, none has presented itself to our minds in which we could classify the poetic idea of the solitary savage, happy in his thoughts in the midst of mother nature, such as Rousseau depicted it to himself and to our fathers: – "Je le vois se rassaisiant sous un chêne, se désalterant au premier ruisseau, trouvant son lit au pied du même arbre qui lui a fourni son repas." –[19]

But this placid kingdom of thought is impossible in the perennial need and agitation of savage life. Rousseau had accepted the tradition, which unfortunately is plausible, that the aboriginals in Italy had lived off acorns; indeed, analysis of our native flora suggests this unappealing tradition may not have so far wide of the mark. Indeed, the same tradition populated the woods of Italy and Greece with the grim semblances of the Laestrygonians, Cyclops, Cacus, Lycaon and Thyestes.[20] These were the confused memories of the past that included the ghosts of cannibal life. And this was inevitable for as long as the naked aboriginal, in the deserted woods of oaks and ilexes, living without a house, fishing without a net, hunting without weapons, had to have something to satisfy his appetite regularly every day of the year, without knowing how to protect the uncertain prey and short-lived fruits from the excesses of the elements and the dangers of both nocturnal and diurnal animals. Satiated and weighed down by food today, tomorrow reduced to gnawing the rotten leftovers – either to die of hunger – or to remain alive by devouring the corpse of one of his peers. For this reason, in certain countries in southern Africa, when someone kills a large animal, ancient tradition requires that the whole tribe should hurry to share it with him; and whoever in turn betrays the exchange is cursed by sacred oaths, to the justice of which each subsequent calamity is attributed.

Hence if Hobbes defined savage man as a *puer robustus*, it would in fact be more accurate to describe him as a *puer famelicus*; because that perpetual anxiety of life would at the same time be indicated as the cause of this perpetual *puerility of the mind*.

---

[19] Cattaneo owned a copy of Rousseau's complete works (*Oeuvres complètes de J.J. Rousseau, citoyen de Genève* (Aux Deux-Ponts: Sanson, 1792-93), 33 vols; cf. BC, n. 1580). The quotation here, which is taken from Rousseau's *Discours sur l'origine et les fondements de l'inégalité parmi les hommes*, is also quoted by Cattaneo in his "Ideologia delle genti, Delle idee nei popoli selvaggi", SF, III, pp. 13ff., where he again rejects Rousseau's theory. (Translator's note: "I see him satisfying his hunger under an oak tree, his thirst at the next rivulet, and reposing after his repast at the very identical spot where he had enjoyed it", in *An Ethical Treatise on the Passions, founded on the Principles Investigated in the Philosophical Treatise*, trans. by T. Cogan (Bath: Hazard and Binns, 1807), p. 484.)

[20] Mythological characters, described at greater length by Cattaneo in "Ideologia delle genti, Delle idee nei popoli selvaggi", SF, III, pp. 4ff., where he deals with the issue of cannibalism.

Lecture VI – On Analysis in Associated Minds – Part 2

It may seem to you, gentlemen, that I have digressed too far in searching for those most intimate secrets of the scientific life in extreme barbarianism. But this analysis of the life of thought in its initial simplicity proves useful, for once its laws have been clarified, it will be possible to follow it in its more complex developments.

As the traditions of the individual tribes expanded their currents unequally over the course of the centuries, they still had to meet up and converge at some point. The nearest tribes, either because they were friendly or hostile, had to be mastered by example, by the dominant force of offence. The bow and sling were in those times what the Prussian rifle is today.[21] Perish, or imitate; perish, or accept an idea!

Primitive communications must have been easier and more immediate in the valleys of the great rivers in the more temperate regions; for these offer a long sequence of fertile locations where plants and animals can find nourishment in the soil and waters; and so the tribes find life less uncertain and arduous; where they can multiply and protect themselves in greater numbers; bring together the fragments of their initial traditions amid the *mediating languages* prevailing in such places; appropriate them with new inflections and compounds and metaphors to express increasingly high levels of analysis; attempt the first abstractions of number, time, space and form. Powers of observation are no longer constrained by the inexorable needs brought about by perpetual famine. Acts of attention grow increasingly liberal; the field of attention grows ever wider. Peoples can also move from place to place more easily, gleaning a greater number of local discoveries. This increases the ease of life, the expansion of societies. The work of society begins once again, but no longer is it that of the solitary tribe; rather, it is the tradition of a people living a better life. People begin *to have time*. This is what the Romans call *otium*, or leisure; *otium studio*, leisure for study, as Cicero described it, that is, rest and thought. *Otium* in Greek is called *scholê*, and it is one of the wisest words in that wise tongue. The *scola*, that is, the *otium* of Athens is the portico, the vegetable garden, the groves of Academe.[22] It is the free and pleasant course of the mind in search of the truth.

> atque inter silvas Academi quaerere verum. Hor.[23]

---

[21] The reference is to the war between the Italian-Prussian alliance and Austria, June-July 1866.

[22] Academus was an Attic hero in Greek mythology who gave his name to the "Academe" (or "Academia"), the name of the garden or grove near ancient Athens where Plato supposedly taught his philosophy students.

[23] Horace, *Epistulae*, II, 2, 45. (Translator's note: "and to hunt for truth in the groves of Academe"; *Horace, Satires. Epistles. The Art of Poetry*, trans. by H. Rushton Fairclough (Cambridge, MA: Harvard University Press, Loeb Classical Library vol. 194, 1926); *Epistles* II, pp. 426-27.)

The largest aggregations of peoples took place in the East, along the great rivers where, right from the outset, the native flora and fauna embraced certain key elements of agriculture and sheep farming. Such was the low valley flooded so regularly by the Nile; such were the two rivers of Mesopotamia; the two rivers of Bactria; the two rivers of India; the two rivers of China.[24] In the Tropics, the great associations of peoples took place on the vast plateaus of Ethiopia, Peru and Mexico, for in such places the altitude, amid the snowy peaks, mitigated the heat caused by their latitude. The least favoured land of all was *Australia*, for nature denied it great rivers and fertile plateaus, bestowing on it, rather, an equally thankless flora and fauna. The work of *nature* thus failing, so too, did the work of *society*. The life of thought was impossible. Hence, if we admit the theory of *the common nature of nations*, and the incontrovertible principle of the *common nature of the intellect* even in these miserable excuses for men, it becomes easy to explain how they never managed to grasp the main idea of agriculture, sheep farming, navigation and metallurgy, how they failed to display even the beaver's instinct for construction, and how very probably they are destined to perish amid the corpse-like inertia of a mind that is stillborn.

Gentlemen, I have sought to demonstrate how the origin of ideas is not as simple as the nature of the intellect, and that it cannot be explained only by reference to the nature of the intellect. It seems to me, rather, like a tree which lives with its own life, but which, in order to live, must keep its roots in the earth and extend its branches over civil society.

The generally received wisdom that the main idea of sheep farming would, under normal conditions, precede the main idea of agriculture seems to me unlikely; for this would imply that the two must have been arisen distinctly and separately. A tribe could as easily have found palm or wheat or rice in its country as sheep or oxen, if nature had bequeathed such a gift to them. Even just one of these useful animal or vegetable species would have sufficed to inaugurate sheep farming or agriculture, or both, as the case may be. The man who encountered a wandering flock in some solitary valley in its primitive liberty, needed only to think: *that flock is mine*; and defend it from the wild beasts and his enemies, assisted by his watchful dog who followed him to enjoy the remains of the slaughter. But this would not have prevented him from continuing to collect the wild fruits or some grains or pulses as before. And for agricultural life to begin with one of these, all that was needed was

---

[24] Cf. Cattaneo, "Ideologia delle genti, Del processo delle idee nei selvaggi", on how civilizations tended to develop along the banks of rivers (*SF*, III, p. 26).

for him, in his tribe's centuries of experience, to have reached the point where he was able to make out the seed in that plant which, once it had fallen into the mud, would rise up again as a new plant.

But the pastoral element was more effective in terms of disseminating discoveries, because it was *more mobile*. The tame and gregarious animals were by nature disposed to follow men from place to place and even to *transport them*.

Thus we see the peoples of Asia predestined to move vast distances over the earth and to collect the scattered fragments of savage analysis in all places. The great desert of Africa remained impracticable until the Arabian and Bactrian camel reached the palm-covered oases in this sea of sand.

Now that sustenance was assured and continuous, their thought could finally rise to heaven; and make out not only the sun and the moon; but divide the fixed stars into constellations, and distinguish the planets which accompanied them to one constellation or another. By this stage nature and society had given priority to the treasures of many regions and the traditions of many peoples, ahead of thought. Unfortunately, however, the kind of thought developed by analysis, which proceeds by slow, difficult steps, is overtaken by the rapid flights of synthesis. The imagination is awakened; it anticipates and assumes what it does not know; it runs ahead of knowledge; it exaggerates an idea in order to execute it; it exchanges astronomy for astrology, medicine for magic, contemplation for vision and ecstasy. No sooner did the measurement of fields give rise to the first form of geometry; than the mathematician's science became confused with the art of the fortune-teller: "*Mathematici genus hominum... sperantibus fallax*". Tacitus[25]

While the learned castes in this way exchange hard and faithful observation for vague poetry, the multitudes pass from the misery of the savage to that of the slave. Commerce begins the exchange of commodities; hence everyone specializes in a single trade; flees from the oppressors of their country in search of liberty; flees in order to exercise their trade among other peoples; every trade becomes a secret and new caste; which is what gives rise to that which the economists call the *division of labour*; but which, as far as psychology is concerned, is merely a *new order of analysis*, that penetrates deeper and deeper into the mysteries of nature. Intent only on his own trade, the plebeian passively receives all the general ideas imposed on him by the learned classes. Thus the order of ideas which agrees with the wishes of the power-

---

[25] Tacitus, *Historiae*, I, 22. (Translator's note: "Mathematicians/astrologers…a class of men… deceitful to those who hope".)

ful is encouraged; while all enquiries that could call into doubt those beliefs which the powerful have dictated are repressed and cursed. Analysis proceeds both among masters and slaves; but it is not free, the *powerful set a limit for the others, set a limit for themselves; analysis once again becomes preordained and the result of fate.* In this way power, without realizing it, becomes a limit for power itself. This is what is happening today in Russia, Austria, even France and Italy.

There is a point where official analysis broke free of its chains in the free cities of Greece; but then the Macedonian unity and Aristotelian encyclopaedism came in, followed by the Roman conquest and the Byzantine unity; Greek thought is buried in the memory of the past; throughout the Middle Ages analysis is preordained and the result of fate.

I shall not dwell here on describing facts with which you are more familiar than I.

I shall not dwell here on reminding you how it came to pass that in modern Europe and its colonies, once again in proportion to the more or less free and audacious traditions which they brought with them from their home countries, the power of analysis has been developed to a degree that is unprecedented over the course of the centuries.

You are well aware how universal analysis started to become strengthened with the work of countless orders of special analysis. Quite different from not being able to count the fingers of one hand! – quite different from counting in multiples of five! – quite different from saying two twos and one to mean five, three twos to mean six, three twos and one to mean seven, then not knowing how to go any further, and out of desperation tearing your hair out with both hands and shouting *cuma!* – which means *many!* – in the impoverished language of the tribes which our mutual friend Osculati visited in the forests at the foot of the Peruvian plateau![26] *Universal analysis was strengthened by mathematical analysis*, was strengthened by all the instruments of *physics*, measured all the variations in heat, dispersed the fable of Daedalus;[27] transformed the heat of the fiery sphere into a sphere of ice penetrated in vain by the rays of the sun's photosphere; it weighed the air; calculated the equations for falling bodies; raised up the lightning conductor

---

[26] Gaetano Osculati (1808-94). Osculati's book was contained in Cattaneo's library and indeed features a dedication by the author: *Esplorazione delle regioni equatoriali lungo il Napo ed il fiume delle Amazzoni. Frammento di un viaggio fatto nelle due Americhe negli anni 1846-1847-1848 da Gaetano Osculati membro corrispondente della Società Geografica di Parigi* (Milan: Bernardoni, 1850), (bc, n. 1225).

[27] Reference to Daedalus's son Icarus.

Lecture VI – On Analysis in Associated Minds – Part 2

in defiance of Jupiter Tonans; extended talking wires across Alpine mountain ranges and across the depths of the oceans. It was strengthened by all the artifices of *chemistry*: found the numbers of equivalents, nature's great game of cards, the few cards that make up an infinite series of games; it unmade and remade all the combinations of the kaleidoscope, and calculated other combinations which mother nature herself might not have happened upon; it discovered that all the lethal and vital powers of the vegetable world had not rained down on the earth through the magic influence of the stars, but were little more than numerical proportions of water and carbon. *Medicine* was strengthened by anatomical analysis, it countered poisons with poisons, and used the instruments of death to save lives; this was the meaning of the wise word *pharmakos*, which the early wisdom of the East had brought to Greece.

Turning to the world of *traditions*, universal analysis enquired into all *languages*, exhumed their roots, the roots of their roots; told them with their own words how they were born and how, from the languages of cannibals more brutal than the orangutan and gorilla, they had come to the point of being able to give a classificatory name to all plants and animals on the planet; – to all the stones and petrified creations that had lived in them for centuries and centuries. It took the mysteries of ancient *Egypt* from the humble basalt of Rosetta;[28] it read ten thousand years of dates buried on the walls of the temples and in the bowels of the pyramids. It penetrated the meaning of the wise adjective given to the heavenly vault by Virgil, pupil of the Druids and teacher of Dante:

Terrasque, tractusque maris *coelumque profundum*![29]

Ancient analysis, free at times but always impotent, became free and strengthened; it became irresistible; it is still preordained and the result of fate, but its order is the order of God, its fate the truth. *Freedom and truth!* Gentlemen, write these words on the doors of all universities.

Meanwhile, the ineluctable dominion of traditions, the science of premature and early syntheses weigh heavily over the vast kingdoms of Asia.

---

[28] The Rosetta Stone is a black basalt stele discovered in 1799 north of Rashid (Rosetta) in the Nile delta, containing inscriptions in three different scripts: Egyptian hieroglyphic, Egyptian demotic, and Greek, based on which in 1831 Jean-Francois Champollion was able to decipher the hieroglyphic script.

[29] Virgil, *Georgics*, IV, 222. (Translator's note: "Earth and the tracts of the sea and deepest heaven"; *Virgil's Georgics: A New Verse Translation by Janet Lembke* (New Haven, CT-London: Yale University Press, 2005), p. 67.)

Today, in Europe and the colonies, which have now reached the far extremities of the earth but have not yet succeeding in penetrating all its parts, which have not yet succeeded in recognizing the wealth of mankind throughout all its circuit, the riches and power of the nations is measured against the freedom of analysis: – Science *is power!*

A person who lives parasitically off traditions, or who has not given to science an idea they cannot call their own, is no longer even considered to be a scientist. The art of making the discoveries foreseen and described before time by the prophetic Francis Bacon has spread to everyone. There are now societies of men whose life is concerned with making discoveries; and other men whose life is concerned with announcing them. *This is analysis for analysis!*

We were witnesses of the events which made the destinies of Asia and Africa subject to Europe. Now the greatest of all revolutions is approaching, one which will make all the discordant syntheses of fantastical science subject to the shock of the free, armed analysis of its works; which will finally inaugurate the harmonious freedom of thought for all mankind.

We no longer need to worry about finding the primordial unity of mankind among the relics of the fossil world. Wherever it came from, mankind is proceeding towards the *free unity of thought.*

Gentlemen, this for me is merely a brief chapter; but for others it could become a much longer work.

I already had these ideas in my mind, when, in January 1862, I responded publicly in *Il Politecnico* to the generous request which senator Matteucci, who at the time was a minister, made to me on the reform he was proposing for scientific studies in Italy.[30]

What I proposed to him then as the main principle to be followed in the universities as a whole was the division of labour, that is, free analysis, so that exactly the same curriculum would never be proposed in one university as in another; only the general and necessary sciences, only the preliminary and accompanying sciences would be standard across several faculties; whereas the others would be genuinely *specialist courses* proper to each university. Thus, for example, assuming we had ten standard faculties for engineers across Italy, in each of which there were ten chairs, my idea was gradually to work towards a situation where around half those chairs have a standard curriculum of general sciences equally necessary for all varieties of teaching; while the

---

[30] Cf. Cattaneo, "Sul riordinamento degli studii scientifici", letter to Senator Matteucci (1862) and other proposals on scientific education, *SEI*, pp. 200-59.

Lecture VI – On Analysis in Associated Minds – Part 2

other half would be focused on specialized teaching proper to that university alone. One of the ten faculties of engineers would have to provide specialist training in *pure mathematics*, in order to prepare teachers who are strong in this family of sciences, for the other faculties as well as the high schools and technical and military schools. To maintain a certain local tradition, this faculty of mathematics might be established in Modena. A specialist course for agricultural engineers could be set up in Pavia. In the same way engineering courses in hydraulics, census statistics, marshland drainage, ship-building, railways and mechanical engineering could be assigned to the relevant cities, without forgetting the branch of fine architecture. And I would also add a branch of good and provident rural and urban architecture in its most modest, useful and salubrious form.

Given that in each university these courses would have five general, standard chairs, and five specialist chairs different in each university, with an equivalent outlay in all ten of them we would have five branches of teaching common to all, and fifty specialist branches, all different. Thus this study of engineering which currently, in the ten universities with the expense of a hundred chairs, gives only ten branches of teaching, then, also with a hundred chairs, would give fifty-five branches, only five of which would be standard for all.

If the same principle is applied to the medical, legal, administrative and industrial faculties, there would be hundreds more specialist branches of teaching; and from the combination of all the faculties thus developed, one large proper *universitas studiorum* would arise, as it was conceived when the universities were first instituted with the scarce materials which the Middle Ages had to offer. And instead of miserable, servile, sterile uniformity, Italy would give the example of a splendid national encyclopaedia.

In order to increase the division of labour and the *intensity* of teaching still further, free and occasional courses would have to be admitted in each university by those wishing to bring a new order of ideas. With these free and innovative courses, those aspiring to chairs would be able to make a name from themselves quite differently from the custom of using shortlists, which are consigned to the favours of administrators who are not always competent.

Similarly, the veterans of the faculties who notoriously attend to research activities, giving an annual sample of their discoveries, could cede part of their daily labours and expound on their teachings in *voluntary* lectures open to all.

Indeed, I proposed that a faculty of *New Sciences* should be opened in Rome; and that the most glorious champions of international science should be invited with lofty hospitality to these Olympic Games of thinking Italy. It would be a festival of humankind, the festival of free thought: *Freedom and Truth*.

I concluded on that occasion by saying that: "to every special branch of science a *military appendix* could be added; for young people must always attach a thought of war to each noble thought, like the people lifting their sacred city from the ruins: – unâ manu faciebat opus et alterâ tenebat gladium" (Ezra XI. 4).[31]

---

[31] Biblical reference. (Translator's note: Nehemiah 4.17, "The labourers who carried materials worked with one hand and held a weapon with the other".)

Appendixes

Figure 9 Psychology of Associated Minds. Preface, manuscript's first page.

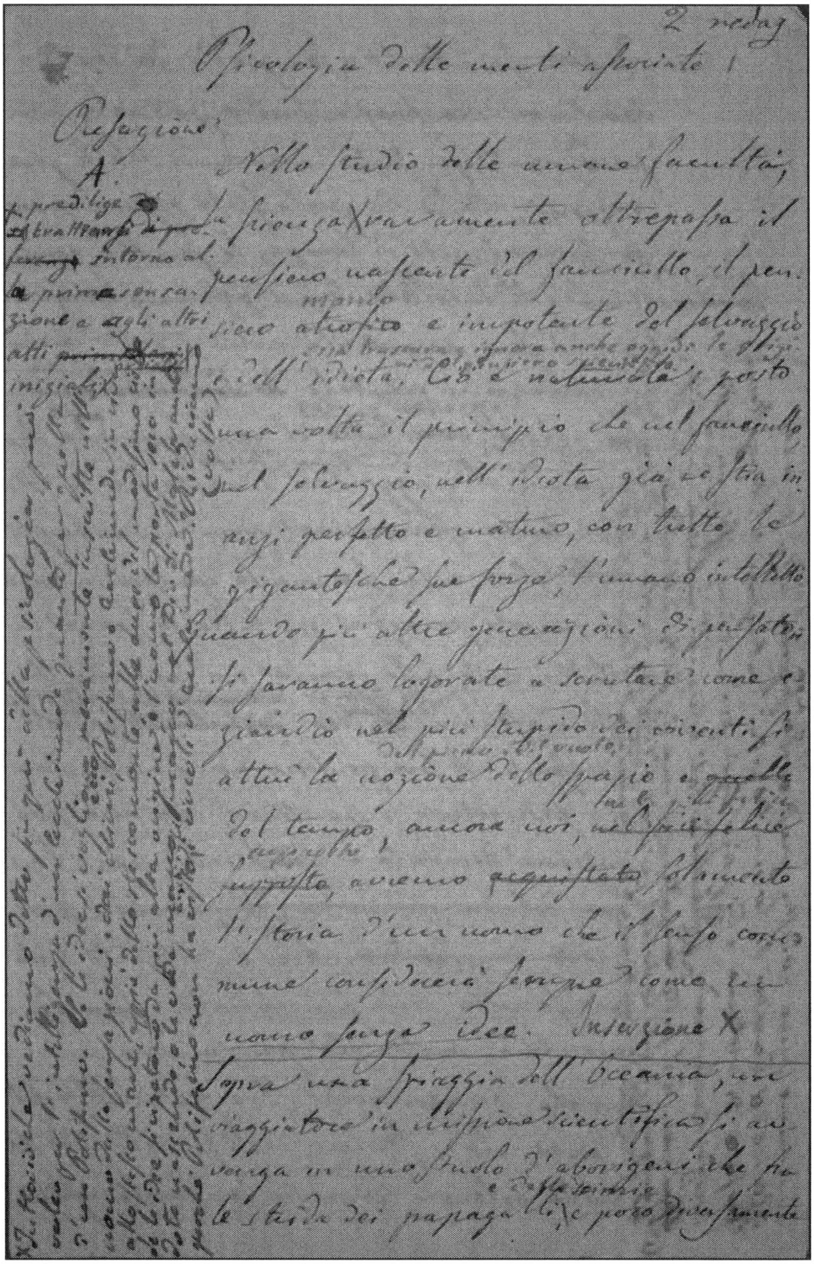

Copyright Comune di Milano – all rights reserved – Milano, Palazzo Moriggia | Museo del Risorgimento

Psychology of Associated Minds
PREFACE

Notes

The undated manuscript is kept in *ACM*. Saffiotti (1882-1927) published a passage from it in 1922, in his *Carlo Cattaneo*, proposing 1855 as a date.[1] The full text was transcribed and published for the first time by Fugazza in "Filosofia e scienze umane: intorno ad alcuni autografi di Cattaneo" (2005).

On the question of dating, the reference contained in this text to a manuscript dated 1855 suggests it must either have been contemporary with or subsequent to the year in question; certainly it appears to predate the lectures themselves but at the same time is clearly related to them, as its introductory nature makes plain.

---

[1] Saffiotti, *Carlo Cattaneo* (Rome: L'Agave, 1922), pp. 42-43 (previously published with the same title in *Il Nuovo Patto*, Rome (1920) III. pp. 10-12, 718-41).

Psychology of Associated Minds
Preface
2nd draft

In the study of human faculties, science prefers to tarry with first sensation and with the other initial acts. Rarely does it get further than the nascent thought of the child; it neglects the truncated and impotent thought of the savage and the idiot; and even today it is ignorant of the origins of scientific thought. This is natural, if we concede the principle that the human intellect, with all its huge powers, is found in the child, savage and idiot already in perfect and mature form. When several other generations of thinkers have exhausted themselves trying to analyse how the notions of solid and void, space and time are played out in even the dullest of living creatures, we will still only have, in the happiest of scenarios, the history of a man who common sense will continue to see as fundamentally *bereft of ideas*.

All that has been said of psychology to date is as valid for the intelligence of Archimedes as it is for that of Polyphemus. If we merely wish to argue that ideas are inscribed in human beings by sensations and climates, we will see Polyphemus and Archimedes on the shores of the same sea, at the foot of the same mountain, by the light of the same heaven. If ideas are merely replicated from a higher source, and if man is endowed with them naturally at birth, or if he comes to see them gradually in Malebranche's God, why did Polyphemus too not see Archimedes' circles? Let us reduce this literary monster Polyphemus to the historical figure of Columbus's Caribbeans or Magellan's Patagonians; by fact of nature and primitive psychology he is no different from Archimedes. If there remains such an abyss between these extremes, it is not due to *nature* so much as to *society*.[2]

On a beach in Oceania, a traveller on a scientific mission happens upon a

---

[2] Cattaneo's note: "Lorsque je vois le soleil, je vois *l'idée* du cercle *en Dieu* et j'ai en *moi* le

host of aboriginals who, amid the cries of parrots and monkeys, and no differently from them, are intent on carrying off the spontaneous fruits of the forest. Such a spectacle, continually renewed throughout successive generations repeated from time immemorial, demonstrates in what state the primitive faculties of the intellect can lay *for an unlimited period of time*. And we can imagine any other people, all of mankind even, closed forever within such a circle of mental operations.

When the traveller, in the same forest, gathers himself to engage in close observation of a particular shrub; and his mind circles in search of remote comparisons among all species of vegetation known to science, we know that he is bringing to bear the fruits of the ideas developed among all thinking peoples. His thought is no primitive or spontaneous phenomenon, rather it is a derivative and artificial production. It did not arise from the faculties of his mind only; *it is the minds of the many who are thinking in him*. Apart from the fact that, comparing the two states of intelligence before us, we see that the chain of ideas which unfolds itself with such agility in the scientist's mind not only could not be reproduced in the minds of those savages, but would also be entirely incomprehensible to them. Their immature speech does not contain the signs necessary for them to be able to distinguish between the elements of scientific classification. Their attention cannot be captured for even a short period of time. Their indifferent, inert mental faculties are unable to take up the invitation: *the minds of others cannot think in them*. Our thoughts cannot be ingrafted into them; it is as though they were plants of a different species. Hence it is not true that science is arrived at by superimposition of ideas, it is not true that *scientiae fiunt per additamenta*.[3]

How can it be that, in the same universe, men who science *assumes* were originally bequeathed with identical faculties in terms of being able to perceive and formulate ideas, should have attained such enormously disparate mental states, that between them there is no longer access to common thought of any kind? How on earth did such insurmountable obstacles arise between them, that the European nations should try not to overcome them and combine their ideas with those of the savages of Pennsylvania and Florida, but should find it more expedient to eradicate them from the face of the earth?

---

sentiment de lumière. Conv.[ersations] Chrét.[iennes].". The quotation is from Nicolas de Malebranche, *Oeuvres complètes* (Paris: De Sapia, 1837, I. 210).

[3] The quotation is from De reactione (1515) by Pietro Pomponazzi (1462-1525). (Translator's note: "science proceeds incrementally".)

Here a twofold series of questions arises. Does the mental difference between two peoples consist of a different *series* of ideas, or a higher *number* of them? Or does it, rather, consist of a different *state* and a *different development of the faculties* that produce them? – Did the mental faculties of the educated people simply produce a higher quantity of labour, as a result of some fortuitous stimulus? Did they merely process a different series of sensations, from a different impulse of external occurrences? Was the mental labour simply accomplished quicker in the civilized individual than in the barbarian one? Was it merely applied to other materials than those found in a woodland environment? – Or is it possible, rather, that the mental faculties among the different peoples perform in ways that are *intrinsically* different? That faculties which were similar originally not only acquired greater force, but also underwent *intrinsic* modification? Could *new* faculties, inaccessible to primitive life, have been activated? – By what impulse in one case is the different and quicker action of the same faculties, or in the other, the activation of superior faculties, to be derived?

Without the faculty of sight, we would never have been able to imagine the phenomenon of light, the presence of the stars; the outer limit of our world would have been as far as the action of our hearing could reach: the surface of the earth, and the lowest stratum of the atmosphere. Whereas, if nature had given our eyes the strength of a telescope, we would also have been able to see the phases of the planets as we see those of the moon. Then, with only a slight effort in terms of reasoning, we would have been able to distinguish their opaque nature from the luminous nature of the stars. This enhanced power of sight would have facilitated our acquiring higher truths. Perhaps in this way the veneration of the seven planets would not, from the earliest times, have concerned the intellect of the peoples who were the first authors of our civilization. – Now, that telescope was not given to us at the beginning by nature but later on, by the genius of man. The person who bequeathed it to us not only increased our faculty of sight, but also enhanced our ability to obtain knowledge of the laws of the universe. He released the course of ideas from those preconceptions that had oppressed it until that century.

Sensation, too, is one of our faculties. Or rather, it is the faculty without which the others cannot be activated; hence whoever increases the effectiveness of even just one of their senses, increases the overall and final effectiveness of their cognitive faculties as well.

Nor was such an increase merely by *degrees*.

It is easy to imagine that, as by nature we had a sense which alerts us to the vibrations of light and one which alerts us to sound waves, so too, we might have been born with other instruments that indicates the way for us, as for example the compass or magnetic influences do. Possibly it is some internal sensory faculty of this kind which directs certain species of rodent in their distant migrations from eastern to western Siberia. The person who gave us the magnetized needle to accompany us through the mists of the ocean, the sandstorms of the desert, or the labyrinths of the mines, thus effectively furnished us with the equivalent of a new sense, no less real than the senses of sight and hearing. It matters little whether it is an organ inserted directly in our temples, or whether, in order to reach our sensory faculties, it has to be represented spatially with the deviations of a needle and translated to the sense of sight; its final effect on the thinking faculties is the same. Through it our mind is initiated into an order of ideas which, more than any other, *is immersed in the arcane mysteries of the universe* and from which primitive man was entirely excluded. It is therefore equivalent to an absolutely new sensory faculty. And it is the work of humans.

Human intelligence also gave our senses other gifts, ones which we have mistakenly become accustomed to consider as primitive gifts of nature. Magellan found tribes in the islands of the Ocean as early as 1521 who did not know what fire was.[4] There is no need to say how many secrets of nature the use of fire has revealed to us, followed by the use of metals. And equally, there is no need to say that the person who gave us the thermometer and pyrometer enabled us to estimate with greater certainty the rigours of frost as well as the heat of furnaces, almost as though our weak hand had been tempered to resemble adamantine.

If those who are scornful of sensation feel the need to cite the artificial increase in other, more profound faculties, it is sufficient to point to the figures of Indian numeration; which, through their powers and decimals, gave us the ability to operate with supreme ease over such huge quantities and such minuscule particles, that without such assistance, our mind would have been unable even to conceive of them. No-one will deny that the ability to perform calculus is one of the sublimest intellectual faculties. If it has remained neglected and virtually excluded from treatises of psychology, it is not because this faculty is not so keenly distinguished from all others. Rather, it is because it is virtually non-existent in the infant and savage, and hence did not appear relevant to those studying intelligence in its rudiments.

Others will say that sublime, or infinitesimal, calculation is attributable to the basest elements of digital numeration, and that in any other branch of mathematics it is always a question of the same faculty, merely at different stages of development.

---

[4] Ferdinand Magellan (1480-1521).

This is akin to saying that an oak derives from an acorn, hence at the different stages of development it remains an acorn.[5] But the transition from acorn to oak offers precisely what is required for the subject matter of research into vegetable physiology and botanical geography. Why does an acorn not turn into an oak on the crest of the Alps? Why does it not become an oak in the sands of the Sahara? In the world of humanity, too, there is, so to speak, a mental temperature at which the intellect was able to generate geometry and calculus; and another one at which this strength was able to lie in hiding for thousands of years; indeed, it could lie in hiding for all eternity, without ever generating the numbers that would be sufficient to count even the fingers of *one hand*. A fine part of our faculties would have remained sterile and unknown. A description of human intelligence in these terms would have been truncated and misleading, for it would have placed us only slightly higher than the brutes; it would have made man a talking monkey. So let them reduce all geometry to merely the idea of space, which everyone possesses; let them reduce history to the idea of time, which all of us have. The annals of science are full of these forced equations. We well know how all mental operations were equated with sensation, how they were all reduced to mere affirmation of the entity. But what was never demonstrated was what new coefficient was applied to the same equations to allow different results to be produced by them in barbarian and civilized men.

The theory whereby compound ideas reduce to simple ideas, and the most sublime speculations reduce to the action of the primitive faculties, does not solve our problem either. If the faculties are equal and constant, it remains to be explained by virtue of which other principle *they may sometimes* be developed to the point of producing compound ideas, and at others *cannot get beyond* the confines of simple ones.

Nor do [inferior][6] ideas differ from superior ones solely as the simple differs from the compound. When man first noticed that the planets appeared first in one, then another constellation, he called them wandering stars; he *saw* them as being similar to living beings that roamed free on the earth. The principle of personality by which he explained the planets' movements, as he had previously explained those of the winds and rivers, ultimately came down to the assumption of their having a will; it was an act of analogy between the planets' nature

---

[5] This sentence, which Cattaneo amended in part, could equally be read as follows: "This is akin to saying that a butterfly derives from an egg, and at different stages of development it remains an egg".

[6] The ms reads: "superior"; probably a mistake, and replaced in the transcription with "inferior".

and that of the brutes, with the human conscience *seeing* a misleading reflection of itself in them. The theory that finally developed in the seventeenth century, which came to see the planetary phenomena as being due to mechanical necessity, was equally an act of analogy, comparing the distant stars to the inanimate bodies that close experience showed were subject to involuntary movement. Long was the ladder of ideas by which science managed to grasp this new point of comparison; but the principle, by whatever route it is reached, if considered in itself, may be ascribed to an idea as simple as, and perhaps even simpler than, personification. At least it can never be said that the primitive idea of personification continued to be included among its elements; on the contrary, it was negated and destroyed by them. The succession of observations revealed that the course of the planets was constrained to follow certain curves and velocities, so that no semblance of free will and life remained. Thus the new idea did not embrace the old one but excluded it; the final act of the mind was no longer a complicated deception but a revelation, not an incremental addition, or *additamentum*, but a replacement.

The principle of personification is *primitive*. Man, although barbarian, was already self-conscious; and so immediately had the ability to *see* the same principle, by analogy, at work in other animals and in all self-moving creatures. All that was needed was for him to note any kind of similar appearance in the air or water, on the earth or in heaven, and he identified his own sentiment with it. Once the idea that all self-moving creatures were volitional had become established, access to any opposite notion became that much more difficult. Hence the new and subsequent principle of *involuntary causes* had to develop slowly, in the shadow of the old one, in the private tradition of the learned, and almost hidden from the poetic conscience of the general public and common sense. I would go as far as to say that the thinkers themselves were unaware of it growing, labouring as they were to develop the ideas from which, at the right time, it would come forth. Faith in the intelligences that governed the spheres continued to prevail not only among astrologers and mystics but also in more sober and robust minds; we see it survive Descartes' vortex theory and Newton's law of universal gravitation.[7] The principle of celestial mechanics was as inaccessible to the reason of primitive man as the planets' atmosphere was inaccessible to his sight. The sequential nature of the discoveries prescribed an order and timescale for the gradual development of the faculties that could not have been foreshortened. A human individual is not born with the ability to improvise so many thoughts.

---

[7] Isaac Newton (1642-1727).

By this I do not mean only that the life of a single man, even if it is a long one, is not sufficient to accumulate all the premises necessary in order to clearly perceive a mechanical principle in the movements of the heavenly spheres. I also mean that even if humanity could have been represented in a single man thinking uninterruptedly, as Pascal rightly said,[8] and if this tireless thinker had been able to compile all the preparatory sciences, he would still not have had the strength to embrace their ultimate consequences. He would still not have been able, suddenly and resolutely at the end of his career, to have banished from his mind that faith in the celestial intelligences with which we suppose he had always lived, and with which all his reasoning was enmeshed and enveloped. It is hard to untangle what has been woven. And even if he had been able to sever all such thoughts with a single blow, how dizzied his intellect would have been at such an unusual order of ideas!

Like a blind man who suddenly opens his eyes and fixes them on the sun's naked light, the inveterate student of ancient superstition would have been dazzled and frightened by the sudden spectre of so much truth. The scientific life of Tycho Brahe,[9] spent in providing arms against the theory that he himself had chosen to defend, is an example of what a scientific life ideally extended to all ages of mankind would be like.

The brevity of life, which cuts off the flow of individual reasoning at any moment, brings with it the compensation at least that the minds of our successors gradually begin a new stage in the flow without affection for past ideas, and without the nostalgia with which intelligences that are waning often look askance at the light that is dawning.

We shall say, then, that ideas that can be revealed in the light of conscience, that is, of internal experience, within that circle of external experiences accessible to the infant, the savage and the solitary, are primitive and inferior. These include the ideas of the self and non-self, of space and time, of solid and void, of forms and dimensions, of pleasure and pain, which have been so explored and chewed over time and time again by the unanimous diligence of thinkers. The ideas we shall call later, progressive, superior, social and scientific are those which can only be manifested in the internal and external experience of *several associated minds.*

This action and reaction of more than one intelligence is truly necessary to development of the moral sentiments. As electrical current is not generated without multiple contacts or without friction, so too, without lengthy consul-

---

[8] Blaise Pascal (1623-62).
[9] Tycho Brahe (1546-1601).

tation and obstinate conflict, man is unable to perceive his rights and duties distinctly; nor can peoples rise up above the animal passions of primitive life. Look at the cannibal, who has still not disappeared entirely from the face of the earth after thousands of years! Consider the stubbornness of that horrendous tradition, which has been able to perpetuate itself in the conscience of so many generations. Then try to avoid this dilemma: either it must be denied that the savage has human nature, or that human nature has all the primitive attributes ascribed to it by the majority of thinkers. By this I mean the Platonic reminiscences, innate ideas, pre-established harmonies, imperative categories, moral inspirations, phases of the entity, emanations of good, and inextinguishable sparks of conscience, which historically and psychologically speaking are only the late discoveries of man himself; who, one degree at a time, *sees* and therefore *feels* himself in his counterpart in every language, faith, caste, sex and colour.

It is one thing that there are rights or duties outside of which man lives as either wretch or tyrant; it is another that he should carry these precepts as though inscribed clearly in his mind. And so, it is one thing that the triangle and circle should have properties that are evident to every intellect that contemplates them; another thing that the intellect comes with intuition gratuitously from its origin.

Let the strictly theological idea which prevailed in the Middle Ages and inspired the work of the inquisitors be succeeded by the largely humanitarian idea typical of the modern period; and you will see if the crowds are still able to enjoy themselves watching the agonies of the Protestant being hauled over burning coals by the executioner. Whatever power is held by a religious tradition, you will see it fall before the authority of the new principle which pushes the bonds of humanity beyond the confines of superstitious beliefs. The highest moral formula is the one which teaches man to consider each of his peers as another version of himself.

Thus we see the *self*, the *ego, egoism* translated to become the ethical measure not only of law, duty and justice but also of charity and love: *Oportet hominem benefacere homini*,[10] wrote the Roman jurisconsult, enlightened by Stoic contemplation of nature and reason. While the *barbarian* or the *barbarized self* restricts all its attention to itself, and its future destiny on earth and in heaven to everything that pertains most strictly to it, the *civilized self* includes in its embrace even things that remind it only distantly of the unity of nature.

---

[10] Translator's note: "it is necessary for man to do good to men".

It is the job of psychology to describe this reversal of the self, this revolution of the conscience. It cannot be forgotten how this new sentiment was aroused in the cannibal ancestor of the nations which began civilization, while the cannibal who survives to this day still does not *see*, does not *feel* himself in the enemy whose blood he drinks and whose members he tortures with such joy.

The laws of society have their reasons in society itself and the coexistence of human individuals, in the same way that the laws of the universe have their reasons in the universe and the coexistence of elementary phenomena. When I see psychology seeking the reasons for the social order outside of society, I see the same mistake as when men moved the blue veil of this low, earthly atmosphere to beyond the stars and turned it into the solid vault of a distant firmament, being repeated in a different order of ideas.

In its research, ancient philosophy did not consider savage man; it did not know him; he was not comprised within the circle of Greek experience. Greek civilization, in its wanderings westwards, eastwards, and also to the south or north, was like a ship sailing from one continent to another, without ever leaving the confines of a single ocean current. The Greeks called Persia, India and even Italy barbarous, and never noticed they were speaking a language that had germinated from the same roots, indelible proof of an ancient communion. Even where languages which came from a different root were such as to announce that the Etruscans, Phoenicians or Egyptians were men of different origins, the unity of traditions was revealed in the affinity of their mythologies. As far as the remote Celts, Scandinavians and Lithuanians, Greece could only encounter expressions of the ancient Iranian people groups.

Aristotle's thought was unable to go beyond the borders within which Alexander's weapons had wandered. The tradition of cannibal peoples being found in the far west by the first disseminators of civilization was hidden among the Homeric fables, for the Greek colonies at the foot of Mount Etna and Vesuvius held no Cyclops or Laestrygonians, but they were able to take root and replace each other in the ancient cities where the Tyrrhenians and Phoenicians had already traded, from the Asian colonies in symbolic figures such as Circes, Medea, and the sirens.

It was only in the age of the great maritime discoveries, in the half century between the first passage of the Portuguese below the line and when Magellan's companions returned to Europe, that the last waves of the Indo-Phoenician current were superseded. The Africans taken to Lisbon from the mouth of the Senegal river, the cannibals found by Colombo in the Caribbean islands, Magellan's Patagonians, the inhabitants of the Marianas islands unaware of even the use of fire, offered a new field of study. But philosophy, closed in the schools as it was, considered them to be degenerations and monsters of humanity, extreme corruptions of the dispersed peoples of Babel, and so continued to limit its study to *normal* man. Bacon never saw the cycle of intellectual experiences. Descartes undertook the study of man in his own conscience; but his first concept was that of a philosopher; the ideology of the cannibal could never have begun from the assertion of thought of which the cannibal is unconscious. His history of the intellect is similar to those universal stories which begin not with the savage earth, but with the empire of Nimrod. He, and those who were inspired by him, refused to make the effort required to explore the origins of scientific thought. They posited the source of every ideal outside of man; some considered ideals to be innate, others the reflection of a divine being, others pre-established functions; in each case man became merely the recipient of an alien thought.

When Vico founded the ideology of the nations, he left out all savage life, explaining it by recourse to an accident, a thunderclap which inaugurated religions, erasing the first woodlands by appealing to agriculture as though it had simply fallen from the skies, rather than been generated by the spontaneous development of savage intelligences. Those who followed Vico on this path always treated the nation's thought as an integral phenomenon, as though it were the work of a single, collective intelligence; they have not yet enquired into individual thought, to discover what contribution it made to the common thought, they have not sought to find out what the effect of social development has been.

We can imagine ourselves closed, within that cloister of ideas forever, not one people or another but the whole of mankind.

Psychology of the Solitary Mind, Second Psychology or the History of Associated Minds

Notes

This is the outline of subjects for study in psychology in which Cattaneo draws a distinction between individual psychology ("of the solitary mind") and social psychology ("of associated minds").

A total of twenty-three subjects are listed by Cattaneo on the right-hand side of the page, beginning with "instinct" and ending with "genius". The points highlight the faculties, means and methods by which thought is conceived and organized, but also, at point 3, a scientific discipline in the shape of phrenology. On the left hand side Cattaneo's ideas for developing and illustrating the subjects are listed numerically, on the right hand side they are summarized with words or brief phrases.

Some of these combinations constitute an embryonic version of the themes which he subsequently developed in the lectures. For example, he writes: "Every new object brings with it a sensation ", which is the theme he will develop in the idea of scientific sensation; "The sciences are associations of ideas. Need for the doctor to be both anatomist and botanist", a theme he will develop in his description of the great analysis; whereas genius, the last item in the list, is associated with the "Brevity of human life repaired with unbroken succession of studies" – the great protagonists of history are not individuals living in isolation, but rooted in society and in the history of human progress.

The text was published by Saffiotti as an appendix to his paper "On the legitimacy of a psychology of associated minds" delivered at the fourth international conference of philosophy held in Bologna in 1911.[1] Saffiotti had graduat-

---

[1] *Atti del IV Congresso internazionale di filosofia* (1911) (Genoa: Formiggini, undated), vol. III, pp. 640-46. Saffiotti, having qualified to teach in experimental psychology, became a university

ed on this very subject, and at the conference expressed his intention to publish some of Cattaneo's unpublished papers, and direct his own studies towards the psychology of associated minds, a branch in which:

> starting from what we might call the spontaneous development of the individual psyche, Cattaneo seeks to investigate: "how, in order to ascend to further orders of ideas, the reciprocal action of several associated minds is necessary, which would hence become the subject of another branch of psychology".[2]

---

lecturer in this subject, making a scientific and practical contribution in the field of industrial and employment psychology. Bobbio referred to this structure, index or programme as the case may be, in *SF*, I, p. LXI, but did not include it. On Saffiotti, cf. Massagrande (2001, pp. 143-50).

[2] Cattaneo's words quoted by Saffiotti here are taken, as he himself indicated, from the lecture On the Formation of Systems (*OEI*, VI, p. 299).

Psychology of the Solitary Mind
Second Psychology or the History of Associated Minds

1. Instinct	Social instincts; imitative musical genius, benevolence, glory,
2. Sensation apparatus of senses	Every new object brings with it a sensation
	Travel and trade
	Instruments; new sensations, measured, comparable sensations (Sun)
	Descriptions
	Who was the American savage that saw the plants of Australia?
	Figures
	Chemical elements. Those which are invisible due to distance, those which are invisible due to size.
	Music, instruments, colours, metals
	unions of men armies, meals
	Oil, wine, vinegar, bread, flour, grains, flock.
3. Phrenology	Crossing of peoples
4. Memory	Monuments and writings
	Certain dates, possibility of knowing causes and effects *from the date*
	Dictionaries
	1. Memory of internal phenomena, ours and others

	2. Intentional memory, non-random, deliberate
	3. On the mobility of memory
	usefulness of dates and reminders to avoid anachronisms
	4. Memory of geological worlds
	5. History of truth and errors
	6. Impressions that have become interesting
	In the solitary mind there is less than the sum of sensations,
	in society the sum of sensations is exceeded
5. Association of ideas (Concatenation)	Proportionate to the higher number of sensations and reminders. Signs.
	Number of half terms proportionate to number of ideas.
	The sciences are associations of ideas. Need for the doctor to be both anatomist and botanist. We cannot think of Jupiter without thinking of Uranus and Neptune, of Turkey without thinking of Mohammed.
6. Imagination madness	Theology
	Poetry poetic types
	Fine arts
	Scientific interest as complementary to ideas due to need to make systems, whole note devoted to studies
7. Attention	Influence of public opinion
	Signs of honour, infamy
	Punishments; exhortations to moral sense
8. Reflection	History of philosophy. Education
9. Analysis	Parts of discourse
	Division of sciences, parallel labour
10. Synthesis	Trade
	Conquest, partial contacts

11. Comparison (in synthesis)	Trade
12. Classification	Proportionate to the meeting of sensations, memories
13. Induction	Multiplication of details
14. Analogy	Imitation Language
15. Causality	
16. Generalities.	Development of mathematics and metaphysics Universals
17. Deduction	Sciences of foreign origin applied to country Calculus
18. Judgements	
19. Hypotheses	Great scientific hypotheses
20. Systems	Religions conquests trade. Making a system with simple truth. System which can never be realized, but can never be demolished. Mixtures of peoples Mixtures of different orders of ideas; tendency to reconcile them, that is, to make new combinations. Greece unable to find modern energies
21. Will	
22. Instinct	like the first impulse for the will
23. Genius	Brevity of human life repaired with unbroken succession of studies. Protagoras

Bibliography

Carlo Cattaneo's very broad bibliography can be found in Giuseppe Armani's great bibliographic inventory *Gli scritti su Carlo Cattaneo, Bibliografia 1836-2001* (Lugano-Milan: Giampiero Casagrande, 2001) and in the update by Giuseppe Armani and Raffaella Gobbo, *Gli scritti su Carlo Cattaneo, Bibliografia, aggiornamento 2001-2005* (Lugano-Milan: Giampiero Casagrande, 2008).

A useful outline of historiography on Cattaneo can be found in "Gli interpreti di Cattaneo da Ghisleri a Salvemini" and Arturo Colombo's "Un bilancio degli studi su Cattaneo da Gobetti a Bobbio" in *Carlo Cattaneo, i temi e le sfide*, Proceedings of the 6-8 November 2001 Milan and Lugano Conference, edited by A. Colombo, F. Della Peruta and C.G. Lacaita (Milan: Giampiero Casagrande, 2004, pp.151-172 and 173-213).

In the following list are included the titles of the quotations and the titles of works on civic philosophy, psychology and scientific thought which are specifically concerned with Cattaneo's Lectures.

Authors are presented on alphabetical order for easier consultation.

Agliati Carlo *et alii*, *Stefano Franscini 1796-1857: Le vie alla modernità*, edited by C. Agliati; Lugano: Edizioni dello Stato del Cantone Ticino, 2007.

Albertoni Ettore A., *Studi Romagnosiani: vol. I, La vita e gli Stati e l'incivilimento dei popoli nel pensiero politico di Gian Domenico Romagnosi, Testo integrale del libro primo "Della Vita degli Stati". Cronologia degli scritti e delle edizioni*, ed. by E.A. Albertoni, Milan: Giuffré, 1979;

— vol. II, *I tempi e le opere di Gian Domenico Romagnosi*, ed. by E.A. Albertoni, Milan: Giuffré, 1990.

Alessio Franco, "Cattaneo illuminista", Introduction to *Carlo Cattaneo, Scritti filosofici, letterari e vari*, Florence: Sansoni, 1957, pp. XI-LV.

Altan Carlo Tullio, "L'ideologia delle genti", in *Carlo Cattaneo e il Politecnico. Scienza, cultura, modernità*, edited by A. Colombo and C. Montaleone, Foreword by G. Spadolini, Milan: Franco Angeli, 1993, pp. 257-265.

Ambrosoli Luigi, *La formazione di Carlo Cattaneo. Illustrata da un'appendice di scritti inediti o dimenticati*; Milan-Naples: Ricciardi, 1960;

- "Carlo Cattaneo e il federalismo", Introduction to *Carlo Cattaneo e il federalismo*, Rome: Istituto poligrafico and Zecca dello Stato, 1999, pp. III-XXXIII;
- "Il pensiero laico di Carlo Cattaneo", in *L'educazione dell'uomo completo. Scritti in onore di Mario Alighiero Manacorda*, edited by A. Semeraro; Florence: La Nuova Italia, 2001, pp. 157-170.
- *Carlo Cattaneo, Scritti dal 1848 al 1852*; edited by L. Ambrosoli, Milan: Mondadori, 1967, pp. XV.

Armani Giuseppe, *Carlo Cattaneo. Il padre del federalismo italiano*; Milan: Garzanti, 1997.

Ascoli Graziadio Isaia, "Carlo Cattaneo negli studi storici. Lettera a Francesco Lorenzo Pullè", in *Nuova Antologia*; Rome: Tip. Nuova Antologia, n. 171, 16 giugno 1900, 636-640; subsequently in *A Carlo Cattaneo nel primo centenario della sua nascita*, Milan: Sonzogno, 1901, pp. 21-22.

Badaloni Nicola, "La filosofia dell'intelligenza e l'associazione delle 'intelligenze'", in *Storia d'Italia, La Cultura, Dal primo Settecento all'Unità*; Turin: Einaudi, 1973, vol. III, pp. 951-958.

Belloni Giulio Andrea, "Cattaneo tra Romagnosi e Lombroso"; Albano Laziale: Strini, 1928, subsequently in *Quaderni dell'Archivio di Antropologia criminale e di medicina legale*, Turin: Bocca, 1931.

Beretta Silvio *et alii*, *Filosofia e Scienze Umane: modernità di Cattaneo, a proposito dell'edizione critica curata da Barbara Boneschi della Psicologia delle menti associate. Le letture di Carlo Cattaneo all'Istituto Lombardo di Scienze e Lettere*, Incontro di studio N. 92, 26 January 2017, edited by A. Robbiati Bianchi; Milan: Istituto Lombardo di Scienze e Lettere, 2018.

Bobbio Norberto, Introduction to Carlo Cattaneo, *Scritti filosofici*, edited by N. Bobbio; Florence: Le Monnier, 1960, pp. V-LVI;
- *Una filosofia militante, Studi su Carlo Cattaneo*, Turin: Einaudi, 1971.

Bolognesi Giancarlo, "Carlo Cattaneo e l'Istituto Lombardo", in *Cattaneo, Milano e la Lombardia*, Incontro di studio n. 28, Milan: Istituto Lombardo Accademia di Scienze e Lettere, 2005, 29-30 November 2001, pp. 93-123;
- "Gli studi filologici, linguistici e orientali" (with Angelo Stella and Maurizio Vitale), in *L'Istituto Lombardo Accademia di Scienze e Lettere, (secoli XIX-XX), Storia della Classe di Scienze morali*, edited by M. Vitale, G. Orlandi and A. Robbiati Bianchi; Milan: Istituto Lombardo Accademia di Scienze e Lettere - Libri Scheiwiller, 2009, vol. III, pp. 3-58.

Bonafede Giulio, "La psicologia delle menti associate di Carlo Cattaneo", in *Atti dell'Accademia di scienze e lettere di Palermo*, Palermo, serie V, vol. VII, anno accademico 1986-87, parte II: Lettere, pp. 9-39.

Borghi Lamberto, "Aspetti educativi e pedagogici nel pensiero di Carlo Cattaneo", in *L'opera e l'eredità di Carlo Cattaneo*, edited by C.G. Lacaita; Bologna, Il Mulino, 1975, vol. I, pp. 175-205.

Brunello Bruno, "La psicologia delle menti associate di Carlo Cattaneo", *Rivista di psicologia*; Bologna, 1925, a. XXI, n. 1, pp. 33-40.

Bucchi Sergio, "Cattaneo 'filosofo moderno'. A proposito della pubblicazione dell'edizione critica della Psicologia delle menti associate", *Il Risorgimento*; Milan: Franco Angeli, 2018, vol. I, pp. 143-154.

Bulferetti Luigi, "Il positivismo liberatore di Carlo Cattaneo", in *Scienza e filosofia. Saggi in onore di Ludovico Geymonat*, edited by C. Mangione; Milan: Garzanti, 1985, pp. 574-589.

Cancarini Petroboni Margherita, Fugazza Mariachiara, Introduction to *Carteggi di Carlo Cattaneo, Serie I, Lettere di Carlo Cattaneo*, edited by M. Cancarini Petroboni and M. Fugazza; Florence: Le Monnier; Bellinzona: Edizioni Casagrande, 2001- 2010, vol. III, pp. V-XLVIII.

Cantoni Giovanni, "Il sistema filosofico di Carlo Cattaneo, conferenza letta addì 8 marzo 1887 al Circolo filologico di Milano", estratto da *Rivista di filosofia scientifica*, Milan-Turin: Fratelli Dumolard Editori, 1887, Serie II, a. V, vol. VI, aprile 1887, pp. 193-205;

– *Scienza e religione*, Milan: Treves, 1870;

– *Campagne e contadini in Lombardia durante il Risorgimento*, edited by C.G. Lacaita; Milan: Franco Angeli, 1992.

Castelnuovo Frigessi Delia, Introduction to Carlo Cattaneo, *Opere scelte*, edited by Delia Castelnuovo Frigessi; Turin: Einaudi, 1972 (4 vols.); vol. I, *Scritti 1833-1839*, pp. VII-LXXX;

– "La città nella storia d'Italia", in *L'opera e l'eredità di Carlo Cattaneo*, edited by C.G. Lacaita; Bologna: Il Mulino, 1975, vol. I, pp. 265-282.

Cattaneo Carlo, *Civilization and Democracy: The Salvemini Anthology of Cattaneo's Writings,* edited and introduced by di C.G. Lacaita and F. Sabetti; Toronto: University of Toronto Press, 2006;

– *Intelligence as a Principle of public Economy, Del pensiero come principio d'economia publica,* Foreword to the American Edition by Michael Novak, Foreword by C.G. Lacaita, Afterword by Marco Vitale, dual language edition; Lanham MD: Lexington Books, 2003;

– "*Psicologia delle menti associate. Le letture di Carlo Cattaneo all'Istituto Lombardo di Scienze e Lettere,* critical edition by B. Boneschi; Milan: Istituto Lombardo di Scienze e Lettere, 2016.

Cofrancesco Dino, *Europeismo e cultura. Da Cattaneo a Calogero*; Genova: Ecig, 1981, pp. 31-5.

Colucci Lauretta, *Carlo Cattaneo nella storiografia. Studi su Risorgimento e federalismo dal 1869 al 2002*; Milan: Giuffrè Editore, 2004.

Cosmacini Giorgio, "Cattaneo, Gall e la frenologia", in *Carlo Cattaneo e il Politecnico, Scienza, cultura, modernità,* edited by A. Colombo and C. Montaleone, Foreword by G. Spadolini; Milan: Franco Angeli, 1993, pp. 267-74.

Cospito Giuseppe, Introduction to Carlo Cattaneo, *La scienza nuova dell'umanità. Scritti vichiani 1836-1861*; Genova: Name, 2002, pp. 9-38.

Croce Benedetto, *Storia della storiografia italiana nel secolo decimonono*; Bari: Laterza, 1921, II, pp. 9-17.

De Liguori Girolamo, Introduction to C. Cattaneo, *Psicologia delle menti associate*, Rome: Editori Riuniti, 2000, pp. 7-36.

Della Peruta Franco, *Carlo Cattaneo politico*; Milan: Franco Angeli, 2001.

De Mauro Tullio, "Cattaneo e il linguaggio", in *Carlo Cattaneo. I temi e le sfide*, Proceedings of the 6-8 November 2001 Milan and Lugano Conference, edited by A. Colombo, F. Della Peruta and C.G. Lacaita; Milan: Giampiero Casagrande, 2004, pp. 133-150.

Di Giovanni Piero, "Carlo Cattaneo: filosofia civile e psicologia delle menti associate" in *Filosofia e psicologia nel positivismo italiano*; Roma-Bari: Laterza, 2007.

Doise Willlem, "Lo sviluppo sociale dell'intelligenza: prospettiva storica", in Gabriel Mugny, Felice Carugati *et alii*, *Psicologia sociale dello sviluppo cognitivo*; Florence: Giunti, 1987, pp, 37-38;

— "Psicologia sociale", in *Enciclopedia delle scienze sociali*, Treccani, 1997, http://www.treccani.it/enciclopedia/elenco-opere/Enciclopedia_delle_scienze_sociali.

Focher Ferruccio, Introduction to Carlo Cattaneo, *L'uomo e la storia. Storiografia, filosofia della storia, antropologia. Carlo Cattaneo*, edited by F. Focher; Milan: Mursia, 1973, pp. 5-40;

— "Cattaneo storico e filosofo della storia", in *Annali della Biblioteca statale e Libreria civica di Cremona*, vol. XXXVII/2,1986, Cremona, 1987.

Fornaca Remo, *Filosofia, politica e educazione in Carlo Cattaneo*; Rome: Armando, 1963.

Francioni Gianni, "Cattaneo illuminista" in *Filosofia e Scienze Umane: modernità di Cattaneo, a proposito dell'edizione critica curata da Barbara Boneschi della Psicologia delle menti associate. Le letture di Carlo Cattaneo all'Istituto Lombardo di Scienze e Lettere, Incontro di studio N. 92*, Milano, 26 gennaio 2017, edited by A. Robbiati Bianchi; Milan: Istituto Lombardo di Scienze e Lettere, 2018, pp. 13-24.

Fubini Mario, "Introduzione alla lettura del Cattaneo" in *Romanticismo italiano*, Rome-Bari: Laterza, 1971, cap. X, pp. 241-248; edited before under the pseudonym of Mario Fusi as afterword to *Lombardia antica e moderna*; Florence: Sansoni, 1943).

Fugazza Mariachiara, *Carlo Cattaneo. Scienza e società 1850-1868*; Milan: Franco Angeli, 1989;

— "Le scienze umane", in *Carlo Cattaneo e il Politecnico. Scienza, cultura, modernità*, edited by A. Colombo and C. Montaleone, Foreword by G. Spadolini, Milan: Franco Angeli, 1993, pp. 37-57;

— "Filosofia e scienze umane: intorno ad alcuni autografi di Cattaneo", in *Cattaneo, Milano e la Lombardia*, Incontro di studio N. 28, Milan, 29-30 November 2001, Milan: Istituto Lombardo Accademia di Scienze e Lettere, 2005, pp. 191-244;

- "Poligenismo e ineguaglianza delle 'razze' umane", *Nuova Antologia*, Florence: Le Monnier, luglio-settembre 2015, pp. 329-36;
- "Il progetto della psicologia delle menti associate", in *Filosofia e Scienze Umane: modernità di Cattaneo, a proposito dell'edizione critica curata da Barbara Boneschi della Psicologia delle menti associate. Le letture di Carlo Cattaneo all'Istituto Lombardo di Scienze e Lettere,* Incontro di studio N. 92, Milan, 26 January 2017, edited by A. Robbiati Bianchi; Milan: Istituto Lombardo di Scienze e Lettere, 2018, pp. 47-73.

Galasso Giuseppe, Introduction, in *Antologia degli scritti politici di Carlo Cattaneo*, Bologna: Il Mulino, 1962, pp. 3-27;
- "Cattaneo interprete della storia d'Italia", in *Carlo Cattaneo. I temi e le sfide*, Proceedings of the 6-8 November 2001 Milan and Lugano Conference, edited by A. Colombo, F. Della Peruta and C.G. Lacaita; Milan: Giampiero Casagrande, 2004, pp. 457-468;
- "Cattaneo: una visione della storia d'Europa (e altri aspetti del suo pensiero storico)", in *Carlo Cattaneo: federalismo e sviluppo*, edited by C.G. Lacaita and F. Masoni, Florence: Le Monnier, 2013, pp. 83-97.

Garin Eugenio, *Storia della filosofia italiana*, vol. III, Turin: Einaudi, 1966, pp. 1186-90.

Gentile Giovanni, "La filosofia in Italia dopo il 1850. III, I positivisti. Le origini: Carlo Cattaneo (1801-69)", in *La Critica*, 1908, a. VI, 105-124, subsequently in *Le origini della filosofia contemporanea in Italia*, vol. II, Messina: Principato, 1921, pp. 1-27 and in *Storia della filosofia italiana*, edited by E. Garin, vol. II, Florence: Sansoni, 1969, pp. 232-44.

Geymonat Francesca, *Carlo Cattaneo linguista. Dal "Politecnico milanese alle lezioni svizzere"*, Rome: Carocci editore, 2018.

Ghiringhelli Robertino, "La filosofia civile di Carlo Cattaneo ovvero Romagnosi e Cattaneo", in *Carlo Cattaneo. I temi e le sfide*, Proceedings of the 6-8 November 2001 Milan and Lugano Conference, edited by A. Colombo, F. Della Peruta and C.G. Lacaita; Milan: Giampiero Casagrande, 2004, pp. 317-23.

Ghisleri Arcangelo, Introduction to *Frammenti di filosofia naturale (Scritti filosofici* vol. I); Milan: Edizioni Il Risorgimento, 1926, pp. 9-48.

Gobetti Piero, "Cattaneo", in *La rivoluzione liberale, rivista storica settimanale di politica*; Turin: Energie nuove, 1 novembre 1925, n. 39.

Groppali Alessandro, "Carlo Cattaneo e la sociologia moderna", in *Saggi di sociologia*, Foreword by Alfonso Asturaro; Milan: Battistelli, 1899, pp. 93-8.

Ingold Alice, "Savoirs urbains et construction nationale. La ville, au delà de l'État-nation?", in *Revue d'Histoire des Sciences Humaines*, 2005, 1, n. 12, pp. 55-77.

Lacaita Carlo G., "Romagnosi e Cattaneo", *Annali della Facoltà di scienze politiche di Milano*; Milan: Marzorati, 1983, vol. III, pp. 585-616;
- "Cattaneo e le Americhe", in *Tra Lombardia e Ticino. Studi in memoria di Bruno Caizzi*, edited by R. Ceschi and G. Vigo; Bellinzona: Edizioni Casagrande, 1995, pp. 203-19;

- Foreword to Carlo Cattaneo, *Intelligence as principle of public economy, Del pensiero come principio d'economia publica;* dual language edition, Lanham, Boulder, New York, Oxford: Lexington Books, 2003;
- "Viaggio nella biblioteca di Cattaneo", in *La biblioteca di Carlo Cattaneo*, edited by C.G. Lacaita, R. Gobbo, A. Turiel; Bellinzona: Edizioni Casagrande, 2003, pp. 15-85;
- "Cattaneo filosofo moderno", in *Psicologia delle menti associate. Le letture di Carlo Cattaneo all'Istituto Lombardo di Scienze e Lettere,* critical edition by B. Boneschi; Milan: Istituto Lombardo di Scienze e Lettere, 2016, pp. 19-71;
- "Carlo Cattaneo editore di sé stesso", in *Studi per Biancamaria Frabotta*, edited by Beatrice Alfonzetti and Carmelo Princiotta; Rome: Bulzoni editore, 2017, pp. 177-96.

Levi Alessandro, *Il positivismo politico di Carlo Cattaneo;* Bari: Laterza, 1928; anastatic reprint edited by Salvo Mastellone and Arturo Colombo, Scandicci (Florence): Centro Editoriale Toscano, 2001.

Mario Alberto, Foreword to *Opere edite ed inedite di Carlo Cattaneo, Scritti di filosofia* (I), Firenze: Le Monnier, 1892, vol. VI, pp. 5-70.

Martirano Maurizio, "L'idea di Oriente in Carlo Cattaneo", in *Archivio di storia della cultura*; Naples: Liguori Editore, XIX, 2006, pp. 43-70;
- "La filosofia civile in alcuni momenti del pensiero democratico e risorgimentale", in *Momenti della filosofia civile italiana*, edited by G. Cacciatore and M. Martirano; Naples: La Città del Sole, 2008, pp. 147-200.

Massagrande Danilo Luigi, "La prima redazione della voce Cattaneo Carlo della Enciclopedia Italiana. Con tre lettere inedite di Giovanni Gentile", *Il Risorgimento*; Milan, 2001, a. LIII, n. 3, 143-50.

Mazzarello Paolo, "La medicina e le discipline affini nelle pubblicazioni dell'Istituto Lombardo" in *L'Istituto Lombardo Accademia di Scienze e Lettere, (secoli XIX-XX), Storia della Classe di Scienze matematiche e naturali*, edited by E. Gatti and A. Robbiati Bianchi; Milan: Istituto Lombardo Accademia di Scienze e Lettere - Libri Scheiwiller, 2008, vol. II, pp. 565-670.

Meldolesi Luca, *Carlo Cattaneo e lo spirito italiano*; Soveria Mannelli: Rubbettino, 2013.

Minazzi Fabio, cL'ingegno critico-filosofico di Carlo Cattaneo", in *Università degli studi di Lecce. Bollettino di storia della filosofia*; Lecce, vol. XII, 1996-2002, pp. 19-52.

Momigliano Felice, "Il pensiero sociale di Carlo Cattaneo", in *Rivista di filosofia e di scienze affini*; Bologna, 1902, 263-76;
- "Il positivismo di Carlo Cattaneo" in *Rivista d'Italia*; Milan: Società Editrice Unitas, 1920, III, X, 1920, pp. 179-94.

Moos Carlo, *L'"Altro" Risorgimento, L'ultimo Cattaneo tra Italia e Svizzera*; Milan: Angeli, 1992.

Moravia Sergio, "La filosofia di Carlo Cattaneo" in *Carlo Cattaneo. I temi e le sfide*, Proceedings of the 6-8 November 2001, Milan and Lugano Conference, edited by

A. Colombo, F. Della Peruta and C.G. Lacaita; Milan: Giampiero Casagrande, 2004, pp. 111-21.

Mucciarelli Giuseppe, "La metodologia delle scienze umane in Carlo Cattaneo" in *Studi su Carlo Cattaneo, Quaderni dell'Associazione Mazziniana Italiana*, Bologna: AMI, 1971, pp. 7-27.

Paci Enzo, "L'ora di Cattaneo", *aut aut*, 1970; Firenze: La Nuova Italia, n. 117, pp. 7-19.

Panzera Fabrizio, "Carlo Cattaneo nel Ticino tra cattolici e liberali", in *Carlo Cattaneo. I temi e le sfide,* Proceedings of the 6-8 November 2001 Milan and Lugano Conference, edited by A. Colombo, F. Della Peruta and C.G. Lacaita; Milan: Giampiero Casagrande, 2004, pp. 549-61.

Poggi Francesco, *Di Carlo Cattaneo filosofo e in particolare della sua psicologia delle menti associate*; Oneglia: Nante, 1903.

Pullè Francesco L., "Carlo Cattaneo come antropologo e come etnologo", in *Archivio per l'antropologia e la etnologia*; Florence: Nuova Italia editrice, 1902, a. XXXII, n. 2, pp. 157-70.

Puccio Umberto, *Introduzione a Cattaneo*; Turin: Einaudi, 1977.

Rambaldi Enrico I., "Il dibattito filosofico", in *L'Istituto Lombardo Accademia di Scienze e Lettere, (secoli XIX-XX), Storia della Classe di Scienze morali,* edited by M. Vitale, G. Orlandi and A. Robbiati Bianchi; Milan: Istituto Lombardo Accademia di Scienze e Lettere - Libri Scheiwiller, 2009, vol. III, pp. 353-61.

Reggi Giancarlo, "Per una storia culturale del Liceo", in G. Cereghetti *et alii*, *Il Liceo cantonale di Lugano. Centocinquant'anni al servizio della repubblica e della cultura*; Lugano: Liceo cantonale-Bellinzona, Centro didattico cantonale, 2003, pp. 89-148.

Ricci Garotti Loris, "Le "idee" di Carlo Cattaneo", in *Società*; Florence: Parenti, 1958, a. XIV, n. 3, May-June, pp. 521-44.

Romagnosi Gian Domenico, *Scritti filosofici*, edited by S. Moravia; Milan: Ceschina, 1974, vol. II, pp. 19-36.

Rossi Paolo, Foreword to Carlo Cattaneo, *La Società umana*; Milan: Mondadori, 1950, pp. 7-14.

Rossi Pasquale, *Sociologia e psicologia collettiva*; Rome: Colombo, 1904, pp. 126-33.

Sabetti Filippo, *Civilization and Self-Government. The political Thought of Carlo Cattaneo*; Lanham, MD: Lexington Books, 2010;
- "Cattaneo come Tocqueville? La 'riscoperta' di Carlo Cattaneo in Nord America", in *Confronti*, 1-2/2011; www. eupolis.regione.lombardia.it.

Saffiotti F. Umberto, "A proposito di Carlo Cattaneo", *La Critica*; Bari: Laterza, 1908, VI, fasc. IV, pp. 314-16;
- *Sulla legittimità di una psicologia delle menti associate* in *Atti del IV Congresso internazionale di filosofia* (1911); Genova: A.F. Formiggini, [1911], vol. III, pp. 640-646;
- *Carlo Cattaneo*; Rome: L'Agave, 1922.

Saloni Alfredo, Introduzione a Carlo Cattaneo, *Scritti filosofici,* edited by Alfredo Saloni; Bari: Laterza, 1965.

Santucci Antonio, "Intervento su 'filosofia e scienza in Carlo Cattaneo'", in Aa. Vv., *Studi su Carlo Cattaneo*, "Quaderni dell'Associazione Mazziniana Italiana"; Bologna: AMI, 1971, pp. 29-37.

Sestan Ernesto, "Cattaneo giovane", in *Europa settecentesca ed altri* saggi; Milan-Naples: Ricciardi, 1951, pp. 209-42;

– Introduzione a *Opere di Giandomenico Romagnosi, Carlo Cattaneo, Giuseppe Ferrari*; Ricciardi: Milan-Naples, 1957, pp. VII-XLIV.

Timpanaro Sebastiano, "Carlo Cattaneo e Graziadio Isaia Ascoli. Le idee linguistiche ed etnografiche di Carlo Cattaneo", in *Rivista storica italiana*; Naples: Edizioni Scientifiche italiane, 1961, a. LXXIII, n. 4, pp. 739-71.

Veca Salvatore, "Meglio ristampare Croce o ristampare Cattaneo"; Milan: *Corriere della Sera*, 12 febbraio 1989, p. 15;

– "Cattaneo, dalla parte del pensiero umile. Scienza, etica e pluralismo: perché non possiamo dirci crociani", Milano: *Corriere della Sera*; 25 giugno 1989, p. 4.

Vitale Marco, Afterword to Carlo Cattaneo, *Intelligence as principle of public economy, Del pensiero come principio d'economia publica,* dual language edition; Lanham, Boulder, New York, Oxford: Lexington Books, 2003.

White Mario Jessie, "Carlo Cattaneo", *The Contemporary Review*, London, Strahan & Co. Publishers, 1875, XXVI, June-November, pp. 465-86, available online in Hathi Trust Digital Library; Italian version in *Carlo Cattaneo. Cenni*, Foreword by Arcangelo Ghisleri; Cremona: Ronzi and Signori, 1877.

Index of Names

A

Abu Ishak-el-Farssi-el-Isstachri, 6n
Acerbi Enrico, 37
Aesop, 74
Agliati Carlo, 15n
Albertoni Ettore A., 3
Alexander the Great, 142
Ambrosoli Luigi, 2n, 14n, 88n
Anquetil Duperron Abraham-Hyacinthe, 120n
Archimedes, 62, 62n, 134
Aristotle, 142
Armani Giuseppe, 82n
Armellini Carlo, 43

B

Bacon Francis, 10n, 121, 121n, 128, 143
Balbo Cesare, 5n
Barthélemy-Saint-Hilaire Jules, 40, 112n
Battaglia Michele, 40
Beccaria Cesare, 2, 3
Benelli, 68, 68n
Bentham Jeremy, 3, 3n, 5
Bertani Agostino, 15n, 43, 82, 82n
Bigatti Giorgio, 12n
Bobbio Norberto, 1, 15n, 20n
Bolognesi Giancarlo, 30n
Boneschi Barbara, 1, 29

Bonnet Charles, 3, 4, 73, 73n
Brahe Tycho (Tyge), 140, 140n
Brambilla Giovanni Battista, 40
Brenier Anatole, 44
Bucchi Sergio, 32n, 89n

C

Caccini Tommaso (Father Caccino), 75n
Campbell Robert, 42
Camper Petrus, 58n
Cantoni Giovanni, 15n, 20n, 27n, 44n
Cantù Cesare, 75n
Carlo Alberto King of Sardinia, 43
Castelnuovo Frigessi Delia, 20n, 69
Castiglione Baldassarre (Baldesar), 90n
Cavendish Henry, 87, 87n
Cernuschi Enrico, 15, 42, 55, 55n
Champollion Jean François, 127n
Chiusi Giuseppe, 41
Cicero, 123
Clerici Giorgio, 42
Cobden Richard, 42
Cofrancesco Dino, 14
Colombo Arturo, 142
Colombo, see Columbus Christofer
Columbus Christofer, 134
Condillac Étienne Bonnot de, 4, 73, 73n, 85, 89, 90, 98, 105, 121

Condorcet Nicolas de, 5
Confucius, 78, 78n
Constant Benjamin de, 5
Constantine Emperor, 59
Cook James, 121, 121n
Cortes Hernan, 110, 110n
Crosbie Ann, married Woodcock, then Hely-Hutchinson, 39
Curioni Giulio, 81, 81n
Curti Cajo Grano, 81n
Curti Curzio, 81n
Cuvier George-Léopold-Chrétien-Frédéric-Dagobert, 24n

D

Daelli Gino, 45, 67, 67n
Dante Alighieri, 5n, 127
Darwin Charles, 23n
Darwin Erasmus, 23n
De Cristoforis Giambattista, 37
De Giorgi Alessandro, 4n
De Mauro Tullio, 85n
Della Peruta Franco, 14n
Democritus, 75, 75n
Descartes René, 4, 71, 71n, 84, 85, 87, 89, 90, 91, 112, 116, 121, 139, 143

F

Ferguson Adam, 5
Ferrari Ettore, 36
Ferrari Giuseppe, 10, 19, 20n, 39
Ferrario Ottavio, 40, 68, 68n
Fichte Johann Gottlieb, 85, 86, 86n, 89
Focher Ferruccio, 12n
Forcellini Egidio, 120n
Fortis Leone, 54n
Frabotta Biancamaria, 32n
Francis I, Emperor of Austria, 37
Franscini Stefano, 15, 15n, 38, 44
Fugazza Mariachiara, 15n, 23n, 51, 58n, 77n, 105, 133

G

Galasso Giuseppe, 19n, 20n
Galileo (Galileo Galilei), 62, 69n, 75, 75n, 112
Galton Francis, 19
Garibaldi Giuseppe, 43, 45, 67, 68, 68n, 104
Gentile Giovanni, 53n
Geymonat Francesca, 69n, 85n
Gherardini Giovanni, 23n, 37
Ghiringhelli Robertino, 3n
Ghisleri Arcangelo, 96, 105
Gliddon George Robins, 23
Gregory Tullio, 32n
Guillard Jules Achille, 40
Guizot François-Pierre-Guillaume, 5

H

Halley Edmund, 45, 45n, 102
Hartig Franz von, 40
Hegel Georg Wilhelm Friedrich, 86
Herder Johann Gottfried von, 5, 57, 57n
Hobbes Thomas, 5, 122
Horace, (Hor.), 123, 123n
Humboldt Karl Wilhelm von, 85n
Hume David, 5

I

Ingold Alice, 20n

J

Jan Georg (Giorgio), 58n

K

Kant Immanuel, 85, 91

L

Lacaita Carlo G., 1, 3n, 6n, 21n, 32n, 34, 69, 69n
Lagrange Giuseppe Luigi, 105, 105n

Index of Names

Laharpe (or La Harpe) Jean François, 121n
Lamarck Jean-Baptiste-Pierre-Antoine de Monet de, 24n
Lampato Francesco, 39
Lassalle Ferdinand, 86n
Lavergne Louis-Gabriel-Léonce de, 20
Lavoisier Antoine-Laurent, 10, 41, 41n, 87, 87n
Lemmi Adriano, 82, 82n
Leroux Pierre, 111, 111n, 112
Levi Alessandro, 1, 82, 82n
Livy (Tito Livio), 2
Locke John, 3, 4, 12n, 85, 87, 91
Londonio Carlo Giuseppe, 39
Longfellow Henry Wadsworth, 19, 19n, 29, 29n

M

Machiavelli Niccolò, 5, 12, 12n, 90
Madini Antonio, 6n
Magellan Ferdinand, 134, 137, 137n, 142
Maistre Joseph de, 92, 92n
Malebranche Nicolas de, 42, 62n, 134, 135n
Mantegazza Solera Laura, 68, 68n
Mantegazza Paolo, 68n
Manzoni Alessandro, 54, 54n,
Mario Alberto, 19n, 29, 29n
Mario Jessie, see White Mario J.
Martirano Maurizio, 14n
Massagrande Danilo L., 146n
Matteucci Carlo, 26, 46, 128, 128n
Mazzarello Paolo, 99n
Mazzini Giuseppe, 43
Meldolesi Luca, 20n
Melloni Macedonio, 45, 45n
Menini Giovan Battista, 40
Metternich-Winneburg Klemens Wenzel Lothar von, 42
Mignet François-Auguste-Marie, 19n
Mohammed, 74, 148
Momigliano Felice, 53n

Montani Giuseppe, 38
Monti Perticari Costanza, 38
Monti Vincenzo, 38
Montesquieu Charles Louis de Secondat de La Brède and, 57, 57n
Moos Carlo, 15n
Morabito Carmela, 32n
Morton Samuel George, 23, 58n
Mylius Heinrich (Enrico), 41

N

Napier of Merchiston John, 57n
Napoleon, 30, 41
Napoleone III, 45
Newton Isaac, 57, 139, 139n
Nicholas I Romanov Tsar of Russia, 44
Niebuhr Carsten, 6
Nott Josiah Clark, 23

O

Osculati Gaetano, 126, 126n
Ovid, 75, 75n

P

Pagano Mario, 5
Panzera Fabrizio, 82n
Pascal Blaise, 140, 140n
Pio IX, 15n
Pioda Luigi Maria, 46
Piperno Marina, 32n
Pythagoras, 60n
Plato, 62, 62n, 123n
Polli Giovanni, 99n
Pomponazzi Pietro, 135n
Priestley Joseph, 87, 87n
Protagoras, 149

R

Radetzky Johann-Joseph-Franz-Karl von, 43
Rambaldi Enrico I., 55, 55n
Ranke Leopold von, 19n

Rasori Giovanni, 23n, 88n
Reggi Giancarlo, 69, 69n
Reynaud Jean, 111n
Riganti Pietro, 103n
Robertson William, 5
Romagnosi Gian Domenico, 2, 2n, 3, 3n, 4, 4n, 5, 6, 38, 39, 55
Rousseau Jean Jacques, 12, 12n, 92, 121, 122, 122n
Rusconi Carlo, 43

S
Saffi Aurelio, 43
Saffiotti Francesco Umberto, 51, 53n, 133, 133n, 145, 145n, 146n
Saint-Hilaire vedi Barthelemy-Saint-Hilaire Jules, 24n, 112, 112n
Salvemini Gaetano, 1
Sangiorgi Maria Antonia, married Cattaneo and before Cighera, 37
Sanvito Francesco, 21n
Schlegel Friedrich, 5
Sestan Ernesto, 2n
Seymour George Hamilton, 44
Sismondi Jean-Charles-Léonard Simonde de, 5
Smith Adam, 5
Stellini Iacopo, 5

T
Tacitus, 125, 125n
Tasso Torquato, 12n
Tertullian, 92n
Terzaghi Giulio, 42
Thales of Miletus, 60, 61
Thierry Augustin, 19, 19h
Thiers Adolphe, 19n
Torelli Luigi, 44
Tracy Antoine-Louis-Claude Destutt de, 5, 85, 85n
Transon Abel Étienne Louis, 105, 105n

Treves Piero, 63n
Trinchinetti Augusto, 99n

V
Vico Giambattista, 2, 4, 10, 12, 12n, 57, 57n, 59, 61, 61n, 76, 77n, 85, 86, 87, 121, 143
Vieusseux Giovan Pietro, 38
Virgil (Publio Virgilio Marone), 127, 127n
Vittorio Emanuele II King of Italy, 45

W
White Mario Jessie, 29, 29n, 46
Woodcock Brydges (Bridges) Charles, 39
Woodcock Cattaneo Ann (Anna) Pyne, 39

List of Figures

Figure 1 Monument to Carlo Cattaneo, Milan, made by sculptor Ettore Ferrari, 1900   36

Figure 2 Assembly Room of Istituto Lombardo, Milan, Palazzo di Brera (Sketch)   48

Figure 3 Idea of a Psychology of the Sciences, manuscript's first page   52

Figure 4 On the Formation of Systems, manuscript's first page   70

Figure 5 On Antithesis as a Method of Social Psychology, cover page, Lugano, 1864   83

Figure 6 On Sensation, Fragment of a Psychology of Associated Minds, manuscript's first page   97

Figure 7 On Analysis in Associated Minds. Part I, manuscript's first page   107

Figure 8 On Analysis in Associated Minds. Part II, manuscript's first page   114

Figure 9 Psychology of Associated Minds. Preface, manuscript's first page   132